Come to the Wedding Feast

An Eight-Session Course for Training Catechists

Dominic F. Ashkar, PhD

Church of St. Vincent De Paul
900 Madison Ave.
Albany, N.Y. 12208

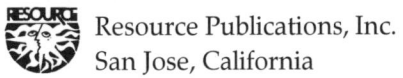
Resource Publications, Inc.
San Jose, California

Nihil Obstat:
Reverend Isidore Dixon
Censor Deputatus

Imprimatur:
Most Reverend William E. Lori, STD
Vicar General for the Archdiocese of Washington

September 27, 1996

The nihil obstat and imprimatur are official declarations that a book or pamphlet is free of doctrinal or moral error. No implication is contained therein that those who have granted the nihil obstat and the imprimatur agree with the content, opinions or statements expressed.

© 1997 Resource Publications, Inc. All rights reserved. Permission is granted to reproduce the worksheet pages for exclusive use within your faith community on the condition of proper acknowledgment. The following symbol identifies the reproducible worksheets :

No otherpart of this book may be photocopied or otherwise reproduced without permission from the publisher. For reprint permission, contact:

Reprint Department
Resource Publications, Inc.
160 E. Virginia Street #290
San Jose, CA 95112-5876
1-408-286-8505 (voice)
1-408-287-8748 (fax)

ISBN 0-89390-400-7

Printed in the United States of America

97 98 99 00 01 | 5 4 3 2 1

Editorial director: Nick Wagner
Prepress manager: Elizabeth J. Asborno
Cover design: Alan Villatuya, Mike Sagara
Production assistant: David Dunlap
Cover photo by Ghazarian Broummana

To my four sisters,
whose life of service reminds me
of Mary at the wedding feast of Cana.

Contents

Acknowledgments. vii

Introduction: How to Use This Guidebook 1

Session 1: The Catechist and Jesus 5

Session 2: The Catechist and Mary 13

Session 3: The Catechist and Miracles 23

Session 4: The Catechist and the Call to Faith 33

Session 5: The Catechist and the Ceremonial Jars 43

Session 6: The Catechist and the New Wine 51

Session 7: The Catechist and the Wedding Feast 61

Session 8: The Catechist and Prayer 71

Conclusion. 79

Acknowledgments

My gratitude goes first to almighty God, who created me and placed me in a family who taught me a deep spiritual tradition, the Syriac Maronite Tradition, not through books and words but through deeds and examples. For many, many years I took this tradition for granted. But more and more I began to understand how uplifting and fulfilling this tradition is for one who allows himself to be carried and fashioned by it.

It is this enriching tradition that leads us on the road of divinization that I will share with you throughout this book. It is like the water of the ocean: It carries us and helps us float without much effort. The various prayers included in this text were inspired by or taken from that tradition.

I wish to thank Resource Publications, Inc., for inviting me to write this book with a view toward offering some help to directors and educators of God's Word. I was asked to write this book as a guide to those who are in charge of educators, to help them use my book *Road to Emmaus: A New Model for Catechesis* as a textbook that will assert and deepen these sessions. I thank God and all who helped and inspired me to offer this book as a tool that will make our journey more biblical and liturgical—in other words, a journey with the Lord.

Grateful acknowledgment is extended to the following for granting permission to reprint copyrighted material:

Scripture selections are taken from the *New American Bible* Copyright © 1970 by the Confraternity of Christian Doctrine, Washington, D.C. 20017. Used with permission.

Introduction

Church of St. Vincent De Paul
900 Madison Ave.
Albany, N.Y. 12208

How to Use This Guidebook

The main purpose of this book is to help DREs guide and encourage their catechists to become more spiritually effective. It is to both DREs and catechists that I dedicate this book as a companion on the walk to Emmaus.

As people of faith, particularly as people with religious responsibilities and tasks, no matter how often we feel that we are in a tunnel or that our faith is so weak it seems to have left us, we must remember Jesus remains with us. We must remember that he is encouraging us and helping us to rise again with enthusiasm, inviting us to journey on with courage. The Bridegroom is with us and he is inviting us to be part of the wedding feast, just as he did in hidden form with the disciples on the road to Emmaus.

The Cana event is an invitation to faith. Engraved upon this invitation we find various people and elements—Mary, the servants, ceremonial jars, water, and wine. They will serve as points of reflection in the coming chapters as the Cana event becomes an invitation to a journey that will connect us with Jesus and the disciples on their journey on the road to Emmaus. To make this connection, there will be numerous references throughout this guidebook to my earlier book *Road to Emmaus: A New Model for Catechesis* as a guide for our study.

This guidebook comprises eight sessions, each a reflection on one aspect of the story of the wedding at Cana that can help religious educators view their task from different vantage points. Each session is structured as follows:

- **Step 1: Opening Prayer** — A prayer is said. Although one is provided for each session, you may modify it or write a completely new one.

- **Step 2: Introductory Remarks** — These remarks, in story form, set the stage for the reflection and discussion around the particular aspect of the Gospel passage for the session.

- **Step 3: Distribute Worksheet 1** — Each of the first worksheets contains the same passage but with different parts emphasized. Remarks and helpful guiding questions are provided for the DRE to use with the participants in small groups to move more deeply into the session theme for fifteen to twenty minutes. Both session worksheets are located at the end of each session.

Introduction: How to Use This Guidebook

- **Step 4: Results of Group Discussion** — A summary of main points raised in group discussion is written on the board or on large sheets of paper so participants may see the results and be enriched by the findings of other groups.

- **Step 5: General Presentation** — Points missed or not thought of during the group discussion are presented. This is the most important part of the session.

- **Step 6: Distribute Worksheet 2** — This worksheet is for reflection, after which the participants write about their thoughts and reactions. Participants will also find the suggested readings for the next session on this worksheet. Both session worksheets are located at the end of each session.

- **Step 7: Sharing and Concluding** — Participants are invited to share their reflections. This is the time for wrapping up the session and encouraging completion of the readings for next time.

- **Step 8: Closing Prayer** — Again a prayer is provided that can be modified or rewritten.

Now that you know the structure of the eight sessions, there is one final thing to be aware of as you use this guidebook: Scholars and exegetes do not specify the exact location of Cana in Galilee where the first miracle of Jesus took place. According to the most recent discoveries, it seems it was actually located in southern Lebanon.

Wherever Cana really is, the event that took place there is a manifestation of the glory of Jesus the Lord—the manifestation of the true light that only eyes of faith can see. The miracle at Cana is a reminder of the outpouring of the light of the Spirit as well as a reminder of baptism, the Eucharist, and marriage.

The Wedding at Cana

On the third day there was a wedding at Cana in Galilee, and the mother of Jesus was there. Jesus and his disciples had likewise been invited to the celebration. At a certain point the wine ran out, and Jesus' mother told him, "They have no more wine." Jesus replied, "Woman, how does this concern of yours involve me? My hour has not yet come." His mother instructed those waiting on table, "Do whatever he tells you." As prescribed for Jewish ceremonial washings, there were at hand six stone water jars, each one holding fifteen to twenty-five gallons. "Fill those jars with water," Jesus ordered, at which they filled them to the brim. "Now," he said, "draw some out and take it to the waiter in charge." They did as he instructed them. The waiter in charge tasted the water made wine, without knowing where it had come from; only the waiters knew, since they had drawn the water. Then the waiter in charge called the groom over and remarked to him: "People usually serve the choice wine first; then when the guests have been drinking awhile, a lesser vintage. What you have done is keep the choice wine until now." Jesus performed this first of his signs at Cana in Galilee. Thus did he reveal his glory, and his disciples believed in him (Jn 2:1-11).

Session 1

The Catechist and Jesus

**Step 1:
Opening Prayer**

Christ Jesus, our Lord and God, you were invited to the wedding feast at Cana in Galilee. There you performed your first sign that created astonishment and called people to faith. Grant us, Lord, we beg you, as we go through our study sessions, that we may understand your Gospel signs. Through your words and signs, may we come to know you and the One who sent you. May we see our vocation in salvation history and the messianic eternal kingdom you came to establish among and within us. Amen.

(You may formulate your own prayer or add to this one:)

**Step 2:
Introductory Remarks**

(Share the following story:)

A college professor was approached by a student who queried, "Conversational ability is crucial for success in my future profession, yet there are no such courses offered. How can I learn the art of conversation?"
"A good question," replied the professor, "and if you will just listen, I will tell you how."
There ensued a long, awkward silence. Finally the student interrupted, saying, "Well, I'm listening."
"You see," said the professor, "you are learning already!"

My friends, we are here to listen to the Word of God. He will inspire us, through the silence of our hearts, with not only what to say but also with what to do and how to live. A short, familiar Gospel text will be distributed to you to serve as the foundation of our monthly sessions. It is the account of the wedding at Cana.

Session 1: The Catechist and Jesus

Step 3:
Distribute Worksheet 1

(Before making copies for distribution, see if you wish to add any questions or remarks to it. Preferably before you distribute it, proclaim the Gospel or designate someone else to do so. Following this, give directives and introduce the questions to be discussed in groups for about twenty minutes.)

Step 4:
Results of Group Discussion

(A summary of the main results of the discussion could be written on the board or large sheets of paper so that participants may visualize the results and be enriched by the findings of other groups. After this summary, move to the next step, which is the most important part of the session: presentation of points the participants might have overlooked.)

Step 5:
General Presentation

♦ The questions raised and remarks made at Cana two thousand years ago continue in our day. Jesus was regarded as a good man but also as one who led the masses astray—a man who spoke with authority but also a glutton, drunkard, and friend of sinners. One day, Jesus approached his disciples, aware that silent questions might have arisen within themselves about him:

> When Jesus came to the neighborhood of Caesarea Philippi, he asked his disciples this question: "Who do people say that the Son of Man is?" They replied, "Some say John the Baptizer, others Elijah, still others Jeremiah or one of the prophets." "And you," he said to them, "who do you say that I am?" "You are the Messiah," Simon Peter answered, "the Son of the living God!" Jesus replied, "Blest are you, Simon son of Jonah! No mere man has revealed this to you, but my heavenly Father" (Mt 16:13-17).

♦ The disciples were "with it." They repeated what they had heard. But Jesus directed the question to them: "And you, who do you say that I am?" Peter, enlightened from above, had the answer Jesus hoped for: "The *Messiah*, Son of the *living God*." This short response summarizes the entirety of salvation history. Jesus is indeed the Messiah, the Son of the living God. He has a mission to bring people to the joy of the kingdom of the living God, and everything Jesus did was in that messianic context.

♦ In our initial reading of the Gospel of the miracle at Cana, we see Jesus as one of the wedding guests. We also see him presented with a request, yet he seems to refuse at first to grant a miracle because his "hour has not yet come."

♦ These are the basic facts, but there is much more. This simple text shows us that although Jesus' time of glorification has not come as it will when he is resurrected and sitting in honor at the right hand of the Father, Jesus does not refuse Mary's request. What he does is place it in its proper context: his messianic mission and glorification after the resurrection.

- Cana is not the only mention of wedding imagery in the New Testament. Jesus Christ is the Spouse of the Church; he calls himself the Bridegroom in Matthew's Gospel (Mt 9:14-15). Later, as he speaks of the kingdom of heaven, he tells us that we are invited to the joyous nuptials but that some refuse or are not garbed in proper attire (Mt 22:1-14). Although the Bridegroom will be taken away (Mk 2:20), his return will occur at an unknown time (Mt 25:1-13). The church is always awaiting that return.

- The church is the new bride. She is the pure daughter of Eve (2 Cor 11:1-3). She must be protected so that she will not be seduced as was Eve. She is to be prepared for the arrival of the Bridegroom, Jesus Christ, the New Adam.

- As the church is the body of Christ, so he loves and prepares her through a bath of baptism and purification (Eph 5:21-32). This purification finds its source in the blood of the cross, by which Jesus gives himself as a pledge (down payment) of his love for her (Col 1:22; 1 Cor 6:11).

- St. John sheds more light on this mystery of the wedding: (1) The apostle presents John the Baptist as a friend of the groom (Jn 3:25-30). He is not the groom but a friend charged to prepare the way for him. (2) John portrays Jesus' first miracle as the manifestation of his glory. But Jesus will celebrate the wedding for which he came to earth when he seals the New Covenant with his blood, claiming for himself the new people that become his bride.

- It is the fulfillment of God's nuptials with humanity that John describes in the image of the wedding of the Lamb in the Book of Revelation. As the paschal lamb, Christ will celebrate his wedding on Golgotha, sealing the New Covenant. Although the Bridegroom has entered his glory and become the eternal liturgy, the journeying church, his spouse, has not yet joined him. The wedding feast is not yet complete, so the church waits and prays in faith and hope: "Come, Lord Jesus" (Rev 22:20).

- The manifestation of Jesus' glory is also a manifestation of his divine power. Jesus performs the miracle at Cana in his own name, reflecting his divinity.

- With the manifestation of Jesus' glory and power, there is the revelation of love. In the simple joy of the wedding at Cana is the reflection of eternal joy.

- Jesus' presence at the wedding feast suggests the wedding feast of the messianic kingdom (Mt 22:2). It also reflects the feast celebrating God's love for humanity. Through Christ's presence at Cana, we see the reflection of the Bridegroom to whom God's love for humanity is bound. The festal wine directs us to the joy of the New Covenant.

- While the Gospel neither relates nor expresses the institution of the sacrament (mystery) of marriage, the Cana event shows the attitude that Christ took regarding marriage and the deep meaning he wished to give

Session 1: The Catechist and Jesus

it. Jesus is the Bridegroom in whose honor the wedding feast of God and his people, as promised in the Old Testament, will be held.

- By his presence at the wedding feast, Jesus shows respect for the marital state. He also provides new wine, symbol of new supernatural love in earthly marriage. The wine that he gives is superior in quality and in quantity to the wine previously served. Marriage is, then, not only the development of and fidelity to conjugal love but also an introduction to a much higher love that gives the spouses the power to love each other with the love of Christ himself.

- The foundation of marriage becomes Christ himself as the supreme Bridegroom. Through the sign at Cana, Jesus reveals how he infuses his own spousal love into marriage, miraculously elevating it to a divine level.

- From this first recorded miracle performed by Jesus, we are placed in that context of manifestation of glory, power, and love that moves us, indeed moves the whole world, onward to the messianic kingdom, the eternal heavenly wedding feast, the eternal liturgy of the Lamb of God.

Step 6:
Distribute Worksheet 2

(After distributing this worksheet, read or select someone else to read the passage, "On a Journey." After reading the passage, read the remarks on the worksheet as well as the activity. Mention the suggested readings for the next session.)

Step 7:
Sharing and Concluding

- Would you like to share any of your reflections or changes you made on your last worksheet?

- Before we close our session with a prayer, I wish to remind you to read the suggested passages. As you read them, keep in mind that the question of Jesus is always awaiting our daily personal answer: "And *you*, who do you think that I am?"

Step 8:
Closing Prayer

O Lord, we thank you for inviting us on a difficult but beautiful journey of faith. We ask you to continue to accompany us, shedding your light so we may contemplate not only your first sign at Cana but also all your signs and witness so we may sing your glory. Help us, Lord, always to find strength in prayer as we become members of your family, the Holy Trinity, Father, Son, and Holy Spirit, to whom is always glory and honor forever and ever. Amen.

(You may formulate your own prayer or add to this one:)

Session 1

Worksheet 1

The Wedding at Cana

On the third day there was a wedding at Cana in Galilee, and the mother of JESUS was there. JESUS and HIS disciples had likewise been invited to the celebration. At a certain point the wine ran out, and JESUS' mother told HIM, "They have no more wine." JESUS replied, "Woman, how does this concern of yours involve me? My hour has not yet come." HIS mother instructed those waiting on table, "Do whatever he tells you." As prescribed for Jewish ceremonial washings, there were at hand six stone water jars, each one holding fifteen to twenty-five gallons. "Fill those jars with water," JESUS ordered, at which they filled them to the brim. "Now," HE said, "draw some out and take it to the waiter in charge." They did as HE instructed them. The waiter in charge tasted the water made wine, without knowing where it had come from; only the waiters knew, since they had drawn the water. Then the waiter in charge called the groom over and remarked to him: "People usually serve the choice wine first; then when the guests have been drinking awhile, a lesser vintage. What you have done is keep the choice wine until now." JESUS performed this first of his signs at Cana in Galilee. Thus did HE reveal his glory, and HIS disciples believed in HIM (Jn 2:1-11).

Remarks

- Notice that the word "Jesus" and words referring to him are in all capital letters, calling him and his role to our attention.

- Using the questions on the back of this page, take twenty minutes in small groups to reflect on this passage of the Gospel.

This worksheet was taken from *Come to the Wedding Feast: An Eight-Session Course for Training Catechists* by Dominic F. Ashkar, PhD, © 1997 Resource Publications, Inc. All rights reserved.

Session 1

Worksheet 1 (*continued*)

Helpful Guiding Questions

- How many times is Jesus named or referred to in the text?

- Who is this Jesus to you personally?

- What main title could you suggest as a response to the famous question of Jesus: "And you, who do you say that I am?" (Mt 16:13-17).

- How is Jesus presented to us in the Cana Gospel?

- Can you identify his humanity and his divinity?

- Where do we fit into the Cana Gospel? Do we have a role?

This worksheet was taken from *Come to the Wedding Feast: An Eight-Session Course for Training Catechists* by Dominic F. Ashkar, PhD, © 1997 Resource Publications, Inc. All rights reserved.

Session 1

Worksheet 2

On a Journey

You have been sent on a journey. You had no choice about when or where it started. You don't know when, where, or how it will end. You have no map. All you know for sure is that it is bound to end sometime.

There are rules that apply to this journey, but you've had to learn them as you go. And you cannot control them. You may not even know the purpose of the journey even though others claim to know.

All you know is that once started, you must continue every day, whether you feel like it or not. You start with no possessions, and when you finish you must turn in all you have accumulated. In the end, say some, you will be rewarded or punished. But how do they know for sure?

That's life, my friends, and you cannot change it. A little faith and a sense of humor, fortunately, help cushion some of the bumps.

— Anonymous

Remark

- My friends, the Messiah we have been speaking of is our travel companion. He is our hope, our faith, and our assurance.

Session 1

Worksheet 2 (*continued*)

Helpful Guiding Activity

- Take a few moments to rewrite the preceding passage with additions or changes that will relate to your personal life. It will be for you to keep.

**Suggested Readings for Our Next Session
(from *Road to Emmaus: A New Model for Catechesis*)**

- "Jesus Knew Who He Was" and "Jesus Knew His Mission," pages 57-73 (related to Session 1)

- "The Solution: Evangelization," pages 13-32 (for our next session)

Session 2

The Catechist and Mary

Step 1:
Opening Prayer

Christ Jesus, our Lord, we glorify you because at your Mother's request, at Cana of Galilee, you made holy the joy of the wedding feast. We ask you to place your joy in our hearts so that through you, and like Mary your Mother, we may always live in faith, call on you in hope, witness to you in love, and give you thanks for your mercy. Please, Lord, give us a taste of your eternal wedding feast so that we may continue to journey with faith and joy. Amen.

(You may formulate your own prayer or add to this one:)

Step 2:
Introductory Remarks

(Share the following story:)

A young man answered a want-ad for a farmhand. He told the owner about his previous work experience and then added, "And I can sleep when the wind blows." This remark puzzled the farmer, but he hired the young man. During the next few months, the hired hand did everything asked of him and the farmer was satisfied.

Late one night, one of those infamous midwestern windstorms roared across the plains. It was two in the morning, but the farmer got up, put on his clothes, and ran out to tie down whatever needed to be secured. First he checked the barn. The doors were shut tight, shutters closed, and the animals properly tied in their stalls. Next he checked the springhouse, the pump, the storage shed, the machinery, and the trucks. All was secured.

Still the farmer ran frantically from place to place. He just knew something had to be loose, uncovered, or rattling. But everything was as it should be, so the farmer stuck his head into the bunkhouse to thank the new hand—only to find him sound asleep. Now the farmer remembered the curious statement, "I can sleep when the wind blows." He smiled, realizing that the young man had done everything he was expected to do. This was why he could, indeed, sleep when the wind blew.

There is a similarity between the young man and Mary at Cana. The young man had done what needed to be done because he was aware of all the needs. In our session today, we will once more read the Gospel text of the wedding at Cana and take note of how Mary, although only a guest, sees what is lacking. She brings the request to Jesus, then seems to ignore his remark and confidently goes to the servants, saying, "Do whatever he tells you." As we read and reflect on this short passage, let us see how we, like Mary, do what has to be done with faith.

Step 3:
Distribute Worksheet 1

(Before making copies for distribution, see if you wish to add any questions or remarks to it. Preferably before you distribute it, proclaim the Gospel or designate someone else to do so. Following this, give directives and introduce the questions to be discussed in groups for about twenty minutes.)

Step 4:
Results of
Group Discussion

(A summary of the main results of the discussion could be written on the board or large sheets of paper so participants may visualize the results and be enriched by the findings of other groups. After this summary, move to the next step, which is the most important part of the session: presentation of points the participants might have overlooked.)

Step 5:
General Presentation

- At this wedding, Mary is the only guest who seems to be overstepping her boundaries by asking for a miracle. She brings the request to Jesus but then seems to ignore his remark.

- There are no arguments, no going back and forth, no pleading or begging. Mary makes a suggestion to her son, Jesus, then continues in the same vein by making another suggestion to the servants.

- Mary asks the servants to trust Jesus. What certainty she expresses that her humble prayer will be effective!

- Mary certainly seems to know who she is and who Jesus is. Even if we might initially think her comment, "They have no more wine," just an off-hand remark, her words show she expected he might indeed do something about the dilemma.

- After making the suggestion, Mary moves out of the picture. We read nothing further about her in the story. She disappears. It is her son, the Messiah, who will be the center of attention, not she. Mary makes the suggestion and directs the attention of people to her son.

- Some view Jesus' response as a reproach, but others—such as Ephrem, Theodoret, and Chrysostom—see in Mary's intercession a generous but overly human sentiment: anxiety to see the grandeur of Jesus become manifest and reflect on her. Still others see his response as setting up a situation that, despite its seeming harshness, would convey a greater blessing.

- At the wedding at Cana, Mary seems to have direct influence on the work of the Messiah in her request for a miracle that would reveal him as Savior. From that moment on, Mary seems to play a role in the future plan of salvation, the formation of the church's life. She plays the role of the New Eve with the ultimate recommendation, "Do whatever he tells you."

- The Cana event also helps us discover the role of Mary in the plan of salvation. Her maternal solicitation, her faith, and her powerful prayer are lessons for us.

- To be Mother of Jesus Christ is Mary's role, her vocation in the church. It is she who gave us Jesus, the fruit of her womb, and she continues to give him to us. We even find Mary mentioned in the eucharistic celebration, more so in the churches of the East than in the Roman church.

- Other than Pontius Pilate, Mary is the only human being mentioned in the Apostles' Creed, for it is through her that the incarnation was accomplished. The Son of God was not dropped down from heaven, nor did he just appear; he was conceived and born. He was joined to the descendants of Abraham. Through Mary, he joined the human race, the children of Adam.

- This ever-virgin Mary is a model of holiness, intercession, and attentiveness to human needs. She is full of grace. She is our Lady and our Mother.

> Upon arriving, the angel said to her: "Rejoice, O highly favored daughter! The Lord is with you. Blessed are you among women." She was deeply troubled by his words, and wondered what his greeting meant. The angel went on to say to her: "Do not fear, Mary. You have found favor with God. You shall conceive and bear a son and give him the name of Jesus. Great will be his dignity and he will be called Son of the Most High. The Lord God will give him the throne of David his father. He will rule over the house of Jacob forever and his reign will be without end."
> Mary said to the angel, "How can this be since I do not know man?" The angel answered her: "The Holy Spirit will come upon you and the power of the Most High will overshadow you; hence, the holy offspring to be born will be called Son of God" (Lk 1:28-35).
>
> Such was his intention when suddenly the angel of the Lord appeared in a dream and said to him: "Joseph, son of David, have no fear about taking Mary as your wife. It is by the Holy Spirit that she has conceived this child. She is to have a son and you are to name him Jesus because he will save his people from their sins" (Mt 1:20-21).

Session 2: The Catechist and Mary

> This day in David's city a savior has been born to you, the Messiah and Lord (Lk 2:11).

- Doesn't this Cana event present Mary as an excellent model for catechists? (1) She sees the needs of the community and does something about them. (2) She brings these needs to her son, knowing him to be the center of life. (3) She tells those who can help to listen to his directives, to do whatever he may say.

- Mary is not only the model of catechists but also the model of human experience: (1) In her active attentiveness and receptivity, she is the symbol of the relationship of humanity with God. (2) In her parenthood, she is the model of dedication to raising children and then giving them freedom to fulfill their own vocation. (3) In her dedicated virginity, she is the model of total dedication of love and service. (4) In her humanity, she will become Mother of all humanity at the foot of the cross, where the consummation of the Bridegroom's nuptials with humanity will finally take place. (5) In her free personhood, Mary engages her life and humanity in a free acceptance to be part of the plan of salvation of God the Father. She lives out her life as a woman with integrity. (6) While acting with tranquillity and certainty, Mary assumes all human values so present in the world at Cana. (7) Above all, Mary should be the model to catechists, inspiring them with the right attitude and words so that God's love may be made flesh again and again, both in their own hearts and in those of their students.

- In sum, Mary's actions are not independent of Christ's. Mariology is christocentric. Mary's feasts, particularly in the Eastern churches, are either attached to or centered on Christ's feasts. The annunciation, for example, is a mystery that expresses the paschal mystery. As soon as the annunciation became part of Christian worship, Mary was made part of the liturgy. What is liturgy if not life in communal prayer? There is no doubt that as the early church grew up and realized its role and vocation, it also realized Mary's role.

Step 6:
Distribute Worksheet 2

(After distributing this worksheet, read or select someone else to read the passage, "The Gospel According to You." After reading the passage, read the remarks and questions on the worksheet. Mention the suggested readings for the next session.)

Step 7:
Sharing and Concluding

- Would you like to share any of your reflections or changes you made on your last worksheet?

- Before we close our session with a prayer, I wish to remind you to read the suggested passage. As you read it, keep in mind that Mary tells us, too, "Do whatever he tells you."

Step 8:
Closing Prayer

Glory to you, O Most High, who left your heavenly dwelling place and through Mary came to live among us to give us a taste of your mercy and the joy of your kingdom. You performed signs that opened our eyes to your heavenly light. We ask you, Lord, to accept our honor and praise for remaining among us through your body and blood, uniting us eternally to your messianic wedding feast that one day we will unceasingly celebrate. Amen.

(You may formulate your own prayer or add to this one:)

Session 2

Worksheet 1

The Wedding at Cana

On the third day there was a wedding at Cana in Galilee, and the MOTHER OF JESUS was there. Jesus and his disciples had likewise been invited to the celebration. At a certain point the wine ran out, and JESUS' MOTHER told him, "They have no more wine." Jesus replied, "WOMAN, how does this concern of yours involve me? My hour has not yet come." HIS MOTHER instructed those waiting on table, "Do whatever he tells you." As prescribed for Jewish ceremonial washings, there were at hand six stone water jars, each one holding fifteen to twenty-five gallons. "Fill those jars with water," Jesus ordered, at which they filled them to the brim. "Now," he said, "draw some out and take it to the waiter in charge." They did as he instructed them. The waiter in charge tasted the water made wine, without knowing where it had come from; only the waiters knew, since they had drawn the water. Then the waiter in charge called the groom over and remarked to him: "People usually serve the choice wine first; then when the guests have been drinking awhile, a lesser vintage. What you have done is keep the choice wine until now." Jesus performed this first of his signs at Cana in Galilee. Thus did he reveal his glory, and his disciples believed in him (Jn 2:1-11).

Remarks

- Notice that this time, references to Mary are in all capital letters.

- Using the questions on the back of this page, take twenty minutes in small groups to reflect on this passage with concentration on Mary in relation to her son Jesus.

This worksheet was taken from *Come to the Wedding Feast: An Eight-Session Course for Training Catechists* by Dominic F. Ashkar, PhD, © 1997 Resource Publications, Inc. All rights reserved.

Session 2

Worksheet 1 (continued)

Helpful Guiding Questions

- Who is this Mary?

- How does the Gospel passage about the wedding at Cana describe her?

- Does Mary seem to know who she is and who her son Jesus is? Why or why not?

- Who is the center of attention in this Gospel, Mary or Jesus?

- How would you describe Mary's request?

- How would you describe the response of her son, Jesus?

- In the story of Cana, how could Mary be a model to catechists?

- Is Mary merely a spiritual model here, or could she also be a model of human experience? How?

- Is Mary's action dependent on or independent of Jesus?

This worksheet was taken from *Come to the Wedding Feast: An Eight-Session Course for Training Catechists* by Dominic F. Ashkar, PhD, © 1997 Resource Publications, Inc. All rights reserved.

Session 2

Worksheet 2

The Gospel According to You

The gospels of Matthew, Mark, Luke and John
Are read by more than a few,
But the one that is most read and commented on
Is the gospel according to you.
You are writing a gospel, a chapter each day
By the things that you do and the words that you say.
People read what you write, whether faithless or true.
Say, what is the gospel according to you?
Do others read His truth and His love in your life?
Or has yours been too full of malice and strife?
Does your life speak of evil, or does it ring true?
Say, what is the gospel according to you?
 — Anonymous

Remarks

- The most expensive Bible in the world serves no purpose if the Word is not lived, both for ourselves and as an example to others. It might as well sit on a shelf or be put in a museum.

- But if you do live out the Bible, it will become a truly living word for others as well as yourself.

Session 2

Worksheet 2 (*continued*)

Helpful Guiding Activity

- Try to describe "The Gospel According to You" in your own way. Could this "Gospel According to You" become a source of life on your journey?

Suggested Reading for Our Next Session
(from *Road to Emmaus: A New Model for Catechesis*)

- "Jesus Knew His Mission," pages 61-73

Session 3

The Catechist and Miracles

**Step 1:
Opening Prayer**

O Lord, at Cana you were pleased to change the water into wine. Everyone saw your power and the disciples believed in you. You gave the guests quality wine as a sign of the wine given to your church to quench the thirst of Adam's children. The miracle was the response to your mother's request. Help us, O Lord, to call on her not only when we are happy but also in difficult times so that she may always lead us to you as the Wine of eternal life that our souls desire. Amen.

(You may formulate your own prayer or add to this one:)

**Step 2:
Introductory Remarks**

(Share the following story:)

There was once a wise and beloved king who cared greatly for his people and wanted only what was best for them. The people knew the king took a personal interest in their affairs and tried to understand how his decisions affected their lives. From time to time, he would disguise himself and wander through the streets, trying to see life from their perspective.

One day he disguised himself as a poor villager and went to visit the public baths. Many people were enjoying the fellowship and relaxation there. The water for the baths was heated by a furnace in the cellar, where one man was responsible for maintaining the temperature comfort level. The king made his way to the basement to visit with the man who tirelessly tended the fire.

The two men shared a meal together, and the king came to befriend this lonely man. Day after day, week in and week out, the king went to visit the firetender. The man in the cellar soon became close to his strange visitor who came down to the basement where he was. No one else ever had shown that much caring or concern.

Session 3: The Catechist and Miracles

One day the king revealed his true identity to his friend. It was a risky move, for he feared that the man might ask him for special favors or a gift. Instead, the king's new friend looked into his eyes and said: "You left your comfortable palace to sit with me in this hot, dingy cellar. You ate my meager food and genuinely showed you cared about what happens to me. On other people you might bestow rich gifts, but to me you have given the greatest gift of all. You gave me the gift of yourself."

My friends, we are all fascinated by miracles when they happen. But the greatest miracle remains the gift of God to us, and through every miracle God gives himself to us.

As we dwell once more on the Cana Gospel passage, this time we will concentrate our attention on this first miracle of Jesus.

**Step 3:
Distribute Worksheet 1**

(Before making copies for distribution, see if you wish to add any questions or remarks to it. Preferably before you distribute it, proclaim the Gospel or designate someone else to do so. Following this, give directives and introduce the questions to be discussed in groups for about twenty minutes.)

**Step 4:
Results of
Group Discussion**

(A summary of the main results of the discussion could be written on the board or large sheets of paper so that participants may visualize the results and be enriched by the findings of other groups. After this summary, move to the next step, which is the most important part of the session: presentation of points that the participants might have overlooked.)

**Step 5:
General Presentation**

- The miracle at Cana is the first of Jesus' signs. A sign is a gesture that has a spiritual meaning. It is a human and historic event through which the action or the presence of God is manifested. Other signs include (1) the multiplication of the loaves, in which Jesus reveals that he is the bread of life; (2) the healing of the man born blind, in which Jesus reveals that he is the light; (3) the raising of Lazarus from the tomb, in which Jesus reveals that he is the resurrection and the life.

   Glory to you, O heavenly Physician.
   With your remedy, you healed our wounds,
   for you are the source of healing
   and bestow your gifts upon all.
   You are the precious pearl:
   those in need traded it and became rich.
   You are a treasure of blessings:
   the poor found it and they rejoiced.
   You are a banquet of celebrations:
   The hungry ate at it and were satisfied.
   You are the vineyard:
   the withered were planted in it
      and they brought forth fruit.

You are the light:
   those who were blind saw it
   and were enlightened.
You are the incense:
   sinners inhaled it and were purified.
You are a sea of compassion:
   those with leprosy were immersed in it and were cleansed.
You are a crying voice, which opens the ears
   of those unable to hear
and they hear his words.
You are the fountain of life
   and you give life to the dead....
   — Prayer of Forgiveness, Maronite Liturgy, Lent

- The miracle of Cana is the inaugurative sign of many more to come. It is a sign that reveals Jesus' divinity and glory, which will remain veiled until after the resurrection. This divine glory will remain hidden in his humanity.

- This first sign at Cana, then, announces in a veiled manner the glory of the resurrection. We need to recall to mind that the last sign Jesus performed before his resurrection was the resurrection of Lazarus, when Jesus proclaimed that "this sickness is not to end in death; rather it is for God's glory, that through it the Son of God may be glorified" (Jn 11:4).

- All Jesus' miracles are a preparation for the light of the resurrection. They also have an ultimate call to faith, as we will see in the next session.

- While the miracle at Cana, the first of Jesus' signs, manifests his glory and causes his disciples to believe in him (Jn 2:11), the real glory of Jesus belongs to eternity. His earthly glory begins with the miracle of Cana. This is why our attention should leave the visible to turn to the author of the miracle himself, the one who came to manifest his glory.

- The miracle at Cana is a beginning; miracles are only a prelude to what Jesus is to achieve in his church. When we see the church's manifestation of holiness, charity, and apostolic expansion, we see Christ's glory expanded.

- The miracle at Cana reflects that the divine power comes to the world to transform and save it. Christ demonstrates this power in a discreet way. Neither the groom nor the waiter in charge knew about it. Spiritual power always operates in such simplicity that even the person who benefits from it often does not appreciate its real value.

- The miracle at Cana shows that Jesus is not indifferent to the material distress that is part of human life. Jesus guides us to eternal life by being ready to save the simple earthly joys. So this manifestation of glory and power is also a manifestation of love.

Session 3: The Catechist and Miracles

- Cana is, then, the sign of the new age to come. The marriage of Christ and the church brings about the outpouring of the spirit of love that in turn ushers in the age of the church. Love of God and love of neighbor are the foundation of the Law and the Prophets (Mt 22:34-40). In the parable of the Good Samaritan, Christ praises not the priest, who is too busy to stop and help the injured, but the common man, who had pity on the victim.

- Only true charity lived in community will produce good fruit of evangelization and of sanctification in our parishes. Such a life is based on Christ's priestly life (Jn 17:20-23). Jesus prays for his disciples and followers to be *one*. Unity, then, is the fruit of love, so that when people see his followers, they may believe that they have seen Jesus. Communal charity is the most powerful witness to awaken faith (1 Jn 4:7-8,12).

- Songs, TV, radio, and movies present us with a disfigured picture of love. Even those trained as disciples show that they have a weak training in love by reflecting a weak gift of self, which, along with the gifts of heart, mind, intelligence, and whole being, is necessary for love.

- Those who prepare themselves for marriage should thus realize that love is the gift of one's total self. This gift is to empty oneself for the sake of others. Didn't Christ present this spiritual union as the goal of charity in his prayer, "That they may be one"?

- Becoming a model of this unitive love makes us—especially the catechist—become the miracle, no longer just speaking about it but living it.

Step 6:
Distribute Worksheet 2

(After distributing this worksheet, read or select someone to read the passage, "A Second-Century Anonymous Letter to Diognetus." After reading the passage, read the remarks on the handout. Mention the suggested readings for the next session.)

Step 7:
Sharing and Concluding

- Would you like to share any of the ideas you wrote in your letter to future generations?

- Before we close our session with a prayer, I wish to remind you to read the suggested passage and more if you wish to. As you read, keep in mind that the greatest first miracle is Jesus' giving of himself to us forever and that he is always searching us out to walk with us.

Step 8:
Closing Prayer

O generous Lord, we beg you to give us of your wine that we might be inebriated by your love as we journey to your eternal wedding feast. May your grace be always with your pilgrim church and her children, who always desire the lasting joy. May your light, O Lord, enlighten the darkness that the world imposes upon us.

May we be always guided to you, O Pure Fountain, so that in turn, we may quench the thirst of our children, who are under our care. Amen.

(You may formulate your own prayer or add to this one:)

Session 3

Worksheet 1

The Wedding at Cana

On the third day there was a wedding at Cana in Galilee, and the mother of Jesus was there. Jesus and his disciples had likewise been invited to the celebration. At a certain point the wine ran out, and Jesus' mother told him, "They have no more wine." Jesus replied, "Woman, how does this concern of yours involve me? My hour has not yet come." His mother instructed those waiting on table, "Do whatever he tells you." As prescribed for Jewish ceremonial washings, there were at hand six stone water jars, each one holding fifteen to twenty-five gallons. "Fill those jars with water," Jesus ordered, at which they filled them to the brim. "Now," he said, "draw some out and take it to the waiter in charge." They did as he instructed them. The waiter in charge tasted the water made wine, without knowing where it had come from; only the waiters knew, since they had drawn the water. Then the waiter in charge called the groom over and remarked to him: "People usually serve the choice wine first; then when the guests have been drinking awhile, a lesser vintage. What you have done is keep the choice wine until now." JESUS PERFORMED THIS FIRST OF HIS SIGNS AT CANA IN GALILEE. Thus did he reveal his glory, and his disciples believed in him (Jn 2:1-11).

Remarks

- This time we find the second-to-last line in all capital letters, calling our attention to this first of Jesus' signs and its effect on his disciples.

- Using the questions on the back of this page, take twenty minutes in small groups to reflect on this passage of the Gospel.

This handout was taken from *Come to the Wedding Feast: An Eight-Session Course for Training Catechists* by Dominic F. Ashkar, PhD, © 1997 Resource Publications, Inc. All rights reserved.

Session 3

Worksheet 1 (*continued*)

Helpful Guiding Questions

- What is a miracle? How do you understand miracles in practical terms?

- Why is this event at Cana called the first sign or miracle?

- How do miracle, humanity, and divinity interrelate?

- Is there any connection between this first miracle and the resurrection?

- Is there any connection between this miracle and the glory of Jesus?

- What unique characteristic(s) would you attach to the miracle of Cana?

- Do you see in this miracle not only the material gift but also a gift of self?

- Do you find any relationship between Jesus' first sign and the catechist?

Session 3

Worksheet 2

A Second-Century Anonymous Letter to Diognetus

Christians are not different from other people by country, language or customs. You see, they do not live in cities of their own, or speak some strange dialect, or have some peculiar lifestyle. Their teachings have not been contrived by the invention and speculation of inquisitive individuals; nor are Christians promulgating mere human teaching as some people do. They live in both Greek and foreign cities, wherever chance has put them. They follow local customs in clothing, food and other necessities of life. But at the same time, they demonstrate to us the wonderful and certainly unusual form of their own citizenship.

They live in their own native lands, but as aliens. As citizens, they share all things with others, but like aliens they suffer all things. Every foreign country is to them like native country, and every native land is like foreign country. They marry and have children just like everyone else; but they do not kill unwanted babies. They offer a shared table, but not shared bed. They are at present "in the flesh," but they do not live "according to the flesh." They are passing their days on earth, but are citizens of heaven. They obey the appointed laws, and go beyond the laws in their own lives.

They love everyone, but are persecuted by all. They are unknown and condemned; they are put to death and gain life. They are poor and yet make many rich. They are short of everything and yet have plenty of all things. They are dishonored and yet gain glory through dishonor. Their names are blackened and yet they are cleared. They are mocked and they bless in return. They are treated outrageously and behave respectfully to others. When they do good, they are punished as evil doers. When punished, they rejoice as if being given new life. They are attacked as aliens and are persecuted; yet those who hate them cannot give reason for their hostility.

To put it simply, the soul is to the body as Christians are to the world. The soul is spread through all parts of the body, and Christians through all the cities of the world. The soul is in the body but is not of the body. Christians are in the world but not of the world.

This worksheet was taken from *Come to the Wedding Feast: An Eight-Session Course for Training Catechists* by Dominic F. Ashkar, PhD, © 1997 Resource Publications, Inc. All rights reserved.

Session 3

Worksheet 2 (continued)

Remarks

- Our own personal witness can be a miracle to others.

- The gift of myself can be the first and greatest miracle.

Helpful Guiding Question

- If you were to write a letter similar to the one we just read, what would you tell future generations? Write in the space below. This will be for you to keep.

Suggested Reading for Our Next Session
(from *Road to Emmaus: A New Model for Catechesis*)

- "Jesus Approached the Disciples in Person," pages 75-77

This worksheet was taken from *Come to the Wedding Feast: An Eight-Session Course for Training Catechists* by Dominic F. Ashkar, PhD, © 1997 Resource Publications, Inc. All rights reserved.

Session 4

The Catechist and the Call to Faith

Step 1:
Opening Prayer

Lord, help us reflect upon your signs and miracles that call us to faith. Your works are wonderful and your gifts are generous. As we walk in your way, O Lord, we are sure to be blessed. Give us the grace to delight in your body and blood, O Christ our Savior, and open our eyes to your light, just as you gave delight to the wedding guests at Cana of Galilee, where your disciples believed in you. Amen.

(You may formulate your own prayer or add to this one:)

Step 2:
Introductory Remarks

(Share the following story:)

A traveler was returning to his home from a journey to a distant country. At nightfall he arrived at the entrance to a vast forest. Unable either to delay his journey or to retrace his steps, he was prepared to traverse the sullen forest when he came upon an old shepherd from whom he asked the way.

"Alas!" cried the shepherd. "It is not easy to point out, for the forest is criss-crossed by hundreds of paths winding in every direction. They are almost all similar in appearance, though all with one exception lead to the Great Abyss."

"What is the Great Abyss?" the traveler inquired.

"It's the abyss that surrounds the forest," replied the shepherd. "Moreover, the forest is filled with robbers and wild beasts. It is ravaged by an enormous serpent, so that scarcely a day passes but we find the remains of some unfortunate traveler who fell prey to it.

"Still," the shepherd went on, "as it is impossible to arrive at the place you are going without traversing the forest, I have, through compassion, stationed myself at the entrance of the forest to assist and direct travelers. I have also placed my sons at different intervals to assist me in the same good work. Our services are at your disposal. I am ready to accompany you if you so desire."

The candor and venerable appearance of the old man satisfied the traveler, so he accepted the proposal. The shepherd held a lantern with one hand and with the other took the traveler's arm. Then they set out upon their journey through the dark forest.

After walking a distance, the traveler felt his strength waning. "Lean on me," said the shepherd. The traveler did so and was able to continue the journey. At length the lamp began to flicker.

"Ah!" groaned the traveler. "The oil is nearly spent, and the light will soon be gone. What will become of us now?"

"Do not fear," consoled the shepherd. "We shall soon meet one of my sons, who will supply us with more oil." Just then the traveler saw a glimmer of light shining through the darkness. It shone from a small cabin by the side of the narrow path. At the sound of the shepherd's familiar voice, the cabin door swung open. A seat was offered to the weary traveler, and some plain but substantial food was set before him. Thus refreshed, the traveler set out again, guided by the shepherd's son.

In this manner, they journeyed on for the rest of the night. From time to time, they stopped at different cabins built along the path. At each stop the traveler obtained refreshment, a bit of rest, and a new guide. With the dawn, the traveler arrived without incident at the farthest boundary of the forest. Only then did he appreciate the magnitude of the service rendered him by the shepherd and his sons. At the very edge of the forest, right before his feet, lay a dreadful precipice, coming from the bottom of which he could hear the roar of an angry current.

"This," said the guide, "is the Great Abyss my father spoke about. No one knows its depth, for it is always covered with a thick fog which no eye can penetrate."

As he spoke, he heaved a deep sigh and wiped a tear from his eyes. "You seem grieved," said the traveler.

"How can I be otherwise?" replied his guide. "Can I look at the abyss without thinking of the thousands of unfortunate people swallowed up in it every day? In vain do my father and my brothers offer our services. Very few accept them, and of those few the greater portion, after journeying for a few hours, accuse us of needlessly alarming them. They disdain our advice and set out on paths of their own choosing. They soon lose their way and are devoured by the serpent, are murdered by robbers, or plunge headlong into the abyss. You see, there is only this one little bridge by which the Great Abyss can be crossed, and the way that leads to the bridge is known to us alone.

"Pass over with confidence," continued the guide. Turning to the traveler, the guide embraced him and said, "On the other side is your true home."

The traveler, overcome with gratitude, thanked his charitable guide and promised never to forget him. He crossed the narrow bridge and discovered that indeed he was now back in his own land. His family was there to welcome him.

Session 4: The Catechist and the Call to Faith

This long story is to remind us of our own difficult journey as teachers who may sometimes feel we too are lost in the large forest. It takes faith, this free gift of God that must be nurtured and strengthened, in order to reach our heavenly home. For this reason, once again we will look at the Gospel passage that we have read several times, the wedding at Cana, and this time concentrate our efforts on the gift of faith.

Step 3:
Distribute Worksheet 1

(Before making copies for distribution, see if you wish to add any questions or remarks to it. Preferably before you distribute it, proclaim the Gospel or designate someone else to do so. Following this, give directives and introduce the questions to be discussed in groups for about twenty minutes.)

Step 4:
Results of
Group Discussion

(A summary of the main results of the discussion could be written on the board or large sheet of paper so that participants may visualize the results and be enriched by the findings of other groups. After this summary, move to the next step, which is the most important part of the session: presentation of points that the participants might have overlooked.)

Step 5:
General Presentation

◆ Jesus' miracles show that he is sent by the Father and that he is the Messiah. To see a miracle is to be called to believe, for it is a call to see the glory of God, glory that can be contemplated in Jesus as true light and life. St. John beautifully expresses this idea:

> At this the Jews responded, "What sign can you show us authorizing you to do these things?" "Destroy this temple," was Jesus' answer, "and in three days I will raise it up." They retorted, "This temple took forty-six years to build, and you are going to 'raise it up in three days'!" Actually he was talking about the temple of his body. Only after Jesus had been raised from the dead did his disciples recall that he had said this, and come to believe the Scripture and the word he had spoken.
> While he was in Jerusalem during the Passover festival, many believed in his name, for they could see the signs he was performing (Jn 2:18-23).

◆ There is a passage from the old temple to the new temple. This time it is a temple not made by human hands. It is of divine origin. This new temple is inaugurated through the resurrection in the person of Jesus.

◆ Although Jesus asks the help of the servants to fill the jars with water, he does so directly and only because of the faith Mary displays. It is Mary's faith that brings her to comment to Jesus, "They have no more wine." In Mary's faith we see a living witness that she believed in his divine power. Her faith did not arise on the spur of the moment. It came from a lifetime of effort. It was the result of contemplating her son and seeing in him God's image and divine power as the Son of God. This faith of Mary's is in itself a miracle surpassing all others. The depth of her faith is clear in what she says to the servants, "Do whatever he tells you." She is certain he is going to intervene.

- Faith and the Cana miracle are bound together. The miracle in turn becomes an invitation to further faith. Yet faith goes further still to an invitation to love, a love that must be totally free with no expectation of material or spiritual benefit. True love expects nothing in return. It has no limit. It is universal.

- Mary's attitude and faith provide our model to bring about the miracle that in turn becomes a further call to faith. It is through long, loving contemplation of her son that she arrives at this kind of faith. In this regard, the following short Gospel passage will be of great help:

    > When Jesus came to the neighborhood of Caesarea Philippi, he asked his disciples this question: "Who do people say that the Son of Man is?" They replied, "Some say John the Baptizer, others Elijah, still others Jeremiah or one of the prophets." "And you," he said to them, "who do you say that I am?" "You are the Messiah," Simon Peter answered, "the Son of the living God!" Jesus replied, "Blest are you, Simon son of Jonah! No mere man has revealed this to you, but my heavenly Father" (Mt 16:13-17).

- Jesus takes time to deepen the faith of his disciples. In a friendly discussion, he asks a question, giving each one the occasion to publicly share his heart's secret thoughts. Having mingled with the people, the disciples know what they are thinking. The disciples tell Jesus some of the main identities the people have suggested: "John the Baptizer, Elijah, Jeremiah, one of the prophets...." Echoing the voices of the people, the disciples reflect a knowledge of their sacred history. But all these favorable answers are not enough for Jesus. He goes into greater depth.

- Like an experienced pedagogue, Jesus creates the ambiance for his main question, for what is of interest to him. "Who do *you* say that I am?" This same question is being asked of us today by the reading of the Gospel, by a friend, or by Christ himself in the quiet, sacred time of our prayer. It is a question we cannot avoid. It requires an answer, an answer that reflects the quality of our faith. Peter said: "You are the Messiah, the Holy One, the Son of God...." The Jews of Peter's time ignored this response. They did not know, as we do today, that God had a Son. For them to say of someone that he was the "Son of God" was simply to signify that he was chosen by God for a certain mission, which also expressed that he was loved by God.

- Christ's question brings a certain light to Peter's heart. In an intuition of faith, supported by the light of the Spirit, Peter guesses, foresees, and knows. Peter, like Mary, realizes that this man with whom he walked and lived is in deep contact with God, that he is unique, the perfect image of God, the Son of God in an unusual way. What will our personal response be to this question of Jesus to his disciples? Will it reflect the same faith as Peter's?

Session 4: The Catechist and the Call to Faith

- Peter discovers the truth of the son of the carpenter of Nazareth. He professes it because the Father has revealed it to him. To have this faith does not mean that someone is more intelligent than others. It is God who gives faith, and his free gift is developed in prayer. That is one way we realize that Jesus is the eternal temple of God that gathers us all in the spirit of prayer to develop his gift of faith within us.

Step 6:
Distribute Worksheet 2

(After distributing this worksheet, read or select someone else to read the passage, "What Is the Greatest Ability?" After reading the passage, read the remarks on the handout. Mention the suggested readings for the next session.)

Step 7:
Sharing and Concluding

- Would you like to share any of your reflections or ideas you made on your worksheet?

- Before we close our session with a prayer, I wish to remind you to read the suggested passages. As you read them, keep in mind that Jesus is always ready to journey with you, even when the forest seems very dense, leading us to the celebration of the eternal wedding feast.

Step 8:
Closing Prayer

Lord, you performed a marvelous sign and invited all people to your heavenly banquet, and your church throughout the world offers the true wine that was pressed at the height of the cross. May this wine continue to fill us with love as we journey toward your heavenly banquet with pure and sincere hearts. Help us, O Lord, to continue to praise you with joyful hearts as we contemplate the great sign you performed at Cana. Amen.

(You may formulate your own prayer or add to this one:)

Session 4

Worksheet 1

The Wedding at Cana

On the third day there was a wedding at Cana in Galilee, and the mother of Jesus was there. Jesus and his disciples had likewise been invited to the celebration. At a certain point the wine ran out, and Jesus' mother told him, "They have no more wine." Jesus replied, "Woman, how does this concern of yours involve me? My hour has not yet come." His mother instructed those waiting on table, "Do whatever he tells you." As prescribed for Jewish ceremonial washings, there were at hand six stone water jars, each one holding fifteen to twenty-five gallons. "Fill those jars with water," Jesus ordered, at which they filled them to the brim. "Now," he said, "draw some out and take it to the waiter in charge." They did as he instructed them. The waiter in charge tasted the water made wine, without knowing where it had come from; only the waiters knew, since they had drawn the water. Then the waiter in charge called the groom over and remarked to him: "People usually serve the choice wine first; then when the guests have been drinking awhile, a lesser vintage. What you have done is keep the choice wine until now." Jesus performed this first of his signs at Cana in Galilee. THUS DID HE REVEAL HIS GLORY, AND HIS DISCIPLES BELIEVED IN HIM (Jn 2:1-11).

Remarks

- Notice that this time the last verse of the passage is in all capital letters.

- Using the questions on the back of this page, take twenty minutes in small groups to reflect on this passage, then come back and report to everyone.

Session 4

Worksheet 1 (continued)

Helpful Guiding Questions

♦ What is the relationship between the miracle of Cana and faith? Be specific in responding.

♦ What caused Mary to tell Jesus, "They have no more wine"?

♦ Was Mary certain that Jesus would intervene?

♦ What is faith, and how is it developed?

♦ What is the connection between faith and love?

♦ Who is the center of our faith? (See Mt 16:13-17.)

♦ Is there any relationship between faith and temple? (See Jn 2:18-23.)

♦ Is there any relation between faith and prayer?

This worksheet was taken from *Come to the Wedding Feast: An Eight-Session Course for Training Catechists* by Dominic F. Ashkar, PhD, © 1997 Resource Publications, Inc. All rights reserved.

Session 4

Worksheet 2

What Is the Greatest Ability?

There are great abilities that people acquire, cultivate, and demonstrate. In the service of God, however, there is one ability that is the greatest ability of all. What is it? Is it sociability? Compatibility? Accountability? Adaptability? Reliability?

The greatest ability is *availability*. If we are not available to God, no matter what other kind of ability we have, our ability is no good. Ability without availability is a liability.

Availability means that there is a sense of preparedness and readiness. There are people in life who are prepared, but they simply are not available.

Sometimes people assume God cannot use them because they do not have great abilities, special talents or gifted aptitudes. They feel they are just ordinary and do not have anything special for God's use. But God never asks about our ability, only about our availability.

— Anonymous

Remarks

◆ The first step to strengthen our faith is our availability to God.

◆ Our availability to people also helps our availability to God.

This worksheet was taken from *Come to the Wedding Feast: An Eight-Session Course for Training Catechists* by Dominic F. Ashkar, PhD, © 1997 Resource Publications, Inc. All rights reserved.

Session 4

Worksheet 2 (continued)

Helpful Guiding Activity

- Write your own story, reflecting your availability to God and to others. It will be for you to keep.

Suggested Readings for Our Next Session
(from *Road to Emmaus: A New Model for Catechesis*)

- "Jesus Made As If to Go Further," pages 93-96

- "He Took Bread, Blessed, Broke and Distributed It," pages 97-103

This worksheet was taken from *Come to the Wedding Feast: An Eight-Session Course for Training Catechists* by Dominic F. Ashkar, PhD, © 1997 Resource Publications, Inc. All rights reserved.

Session 5

The Catechist and the Ceremonial Jars

**Step 1:
Opening Prayer**

Lord, we beg you to place your love in our hearts and your light in our eyes so that we may continue to praise you for your favors upon us and for your signs that reveal to us your love and concern. May you continue to grant us your divine light, that through it we may understand your signs and continue to quench our thirst with your consecrated wine, which we will always carry in fragile but precious jars. Amen.

(You may formulate your own prayer or add to this one:)

**Step 2:
Introductory Remarks**

(Share the following story:)

There was an old man who carried a little can of oil with him everywhere he went. If he passed through a squeaking door, he put a little oil on the hinges. If a gate was hard to open, he oiled the latch. So he passed through life lubricating all the creaky places, making it easier for those who came after him.

People called him "eccentric," "strange," "cranky," "odd," and still harsher names. But the old man went steadily on with his task, refilling his oil can when it became empty. He did not wait until he found a door or hinge in need of oil, then go home to get his oil can; he carried it with him at all times.

There are many lives that creak and squeak and grate. They need lubricating with the oil of kindness, gentleness, and thoughtfulness. Carrying an oil can is one of the main characteristics of Christian life. We are to carry it around with us at all times. Doesn't this story describe the life of every Christian, especially of religious educators?

Session 5: The Catechist and the Ceremonial Jars

Step 3:
Distribute Worksheet 1

(Before making copies for distribution, see if you wish to add any questions or remarks to it. Preferably before you distribute it, proclaim the Gospel or designate someone else to do so. Following this, give directives and introduce the questions to be discussed in groups for about twenty minutes.)

Step 4:
Results of
Group Discussion

(A summary of the main results of the discussion could be written on the board or large sheets of paper so participants may visualize the results and be enriched by the findings of other groups. After this summary, move to the next step, which is the most important part of the session: presentation of points the participants might have overlooked.)

Step 5:
General Presentation

♦ As we read the Cana Gospel, we may pay little attention to the jars standing around in the room. After all, they are only water jars. But their meaning should not be minimized or ignored. For the Jews, these are ceremonial jars with a deep meaning. They serve for purification; thus they represent tradition. Even if these jars are empty, they are a reminder of the tradition of ceremonial washing and purification. When filled with water, they still remind us of this tradition. But when the jars are filled with wine, they give the old tradition a completely new meaning!

♦ The presence of the ceremonial jars at Cana help show us that the old has passed and that the new is here. Now that Jesus is here, the water is changed into the wine of the New Covenant. It is a simple but powerful word that brings this change.

♦ Don't many of us in religious education feel at times, or even most of the time, like empty jars—or at best like jars filled with only plain, everyday water? Don't we feel that our role is, like the ceremonial jars, just to remind people of tradition? Our sinfulness and our weaknesses make us feel that way. But let us listen to a passage from the Gospel that will fill our hearts with encouragement:

> As he stood by the Lake of Genesaret, and the crowd pressed in on him to hear the word of God, he saw two boats moored by the side of the lake; the fishermen had disembarked and were washing their nets. He got into one of the boats, the one belonging to Simon, and asked him to pull out a short distance from the shore; then, remaining seated, he continued to teach the crowds from the boat. When he had finished speaking he said to Simon, "Put out into deep water and lower your nets for a catch." Simon answered, "Master, we have been hard at it all night long and have caught nothing; but if you say so, I will lower the nets." Upon doing this they caught such a great number of fish that their nets were at the breaking point. They signaled to their mates in the other boat to come and help them. These came, and together they filled the two boats until they nearly sank.
> At the sight of this, Simon Peter fell at the knees of Jesus saying, "Leave me, Lord. I am a sinful man." For indeed, amazement at the catch they had made seized him and all his shipmates, as well as

James and John, Zebedee's sons, who were partners with Simon. Jesus said to Simon, "Do not be afraid. From now on you will be catching men." With that they brought their boats to land, left everything, and became his followers (Lk 5:1-11).

- Wouldn't Peter have felt like an empty jar in the presence of Jesus and the miraculous catch of fish? Peter, although very knowledgeable about the traditional way to catch fish, immediately confessed his weakness and nothingness—his emptiness—before the Lord. Jesus, the good teacher, finds his students, the disciples, right in their own daily milieu. He searches out what they are good at, then asks them to render a service in that area. As the crowds press in on Jesus, he asks Peter to lend his boat. But behind this service, Jesus looks for a still greater gift: the gift of self. That Jesus expresses his need is miracle enough of his love for us, but that he allows us to give him something is truly amazing.

- To serve others is to serve Jesus. So, to ask others to render him a service could bring about a change of life for them. Indeed, making the request for this service could express deeper love for them than doing the work oneself. To best bring out this response, two things are required: humility and confidence in others. But how do we ask a service from others? Do we ask because we are lazy or because we would like people to cooperate? Do we ask just so we will have less to do or to give joy to someone? Do we ask from a spirit of superiority or because we really have confidence in the other person?

- Jesus, who in contrast to Peter does not know much about fishing, makes the request of the fisherman: "Put out into deep water and lower your nets for a catch." Jesus is asking the men to do so after an unsuccessful night of work. But because it is he who asks, they lower the nets. In the end, the Word of God prevails.

- How about us? How about me? How often do I say, "Lord, if you say so, I will lower the nets"? The nets could represent many things. They could be a change in my ways. They could be a change of heart. They could be a change in my way of teaching the Word of God or in the way I deal with my students.

- Peter could have said, "I should take advantage of the situation and ask the Lord to stay with me because I am not that good." Instead, he falls at Jesus' knees and says: "Leave me, Lord. I am a sinful man." Peter realizes his sinfulness and nothingness, but he also realizes the divine presence. On one hand Peter feels like an empty jar; on the other, he feels the greatness of the divine presence. Peter had been at the wedding at Cana. He had seen the miracle. He had seen other miracles, including the cure of his mother-in-law. This time, though, a miracle touches him personally. It hits home. Peter feels the divine presence, but he also feels that Jesus is going to ask something and lead him somewhere. He tries to escape like other prophets of old.

Session 5: The Catechist and the Ceremonial Jars

- "Leave me, Lord." "Stay away from me." In other words, "I am nothing but an empty jar, incapable of serving you." Aren't Peter's feelings my own? I am sinful. I am incapable. I don't have enough talent. I lack imagination. I am not popular with my students. I am a sinful person. I am nothing but a traditional empty jar. The same fear also takes hold of the other disciples, but Jesus uses this occasion to elevate them higher. He goes down to their level, using their own language, to elevate them to his level: "Do not be afraid. From now on you will be catching men." Jesus uses this event to teach them as he used other occasions, imagery, and parables.

- Peter had worked all night long, but God is the judge of time and place. Jesus is the only one who can bring about the change in Peter, yet at the same time he needs Peter's cooperation. Peter, as well as the others, gets the message. They leave everything and follow Jesus. These disciples had already been following him, but that day another decision had to be made. Once again they place their confidence in Jesus. Now they leave *everything* and follow him.

Step 6:
Distribute Worksheet 2

(After distributing this worksheet, read or select someone else to read the passage, "My Community Reflects Me." After reading the passage, read the remarks on the worksheet. Mention the suggested readings for the next session.)

Step 7:
Sharing and Concluding

- Would you like to share any of your reflections or changes you made on your last worksheet?

- Before we close our session with a prayer, I wish to remind you to read the suggested passage. As your read it, remember that even if we feel like empty jars, Jesus is capable of filling us with new wine.

Step 8:
Closing Prayer

Lord God, many times we feel like traditional empty jars that once served for something but now stand empty as we feel thirsty and dry. Come, O Lord, and dwell in our souls and be our joy because you alone can quench our thirst and our dryness. Fill us with water and then change it into wine that will quench the thirst of others and give them a taste of the life-giving divine wine. Amen.

(You may formulate your own prayer or add to this one:)

Session 5

Worksheet 1

The Wedding at Cana

On the third day there was a wedding at Cana in Galilee, and the mother of Jesus was there. Jesus and his disciples had likewise been invited to the celebration. At a certain point the wine ran out, and Jesus' mother told him, "They have no more wine." Jesus replied, "Woman, how does this concern of yours involve me? My hour has not yet come." His mother instructed those waiting on table, "Do whatever he tells you." AS PRESCRIBED FOR JEWISH CEREMONIAL WASHINGS, THERE WERE AT HAND SIX STONE WATER JARS, EACH ONE HOLDING FIFTEEN TO TWENTY-FIVE GALLONS. "FILL THOSE JARS WITH WATER," JESUS ORDERED, AT WHICH THEY FILLED THEM TO THE BRIM. "NOW," HE SAID, "DRAW SOME OUT AND TAKE IT TO THE WAITER IN CHARGE." They did as he instructed them. The waiter in charge tasted the water made wine, without knowing where it had come from; only the waiters knew, since they had drawn the water. Then the waiter in charge called the groom over and remarked to him: "People usually serve the choice wine first; then when the guests have been drinking awhile, a lesser vintage. What you have done is keep the choice wine until now." Jesus performed this first of his signs at Cana in Galilee. Thus did he reveal his glory, and his disciples believed in him (Jn 2:1-11).

Remarks

- Notice that this time references to the ceremonial jars are in all capital letters.

- Using the questions on the back of this page, take twenty minutes in small groups to reflect on this Gospel passage.

This worksheet was taken from *Come to the Wedding Feast: An Eight-Session Course for Training Catechists* by Dominic F. Ashkar, PhD, © 1997 Resource Publications, Inc. All rights reserved.

Session 5

Worksheet 1 (*continued*)

Helpful Guiding Questions

- What significance do you find in these jars in the Gospel text?

- What are the characteristics of these jars in tradition? in spirituality?

- What new meaning does Jesus give these jars?

- Is there any resemblance between these jars and the life of the disciples? (See Lk 5:1-11.)

- Is there any similarity between these jars and our own lives?

- How can we help others transform their lives in the same way that the water jars were filled with new wine?

- What is the main requirement for us to allow Jesus to change our lives from traditional jars filled with water for ceremonial washing into jars filled with new wine?

This worksheet was taken from *Come to the Wedding Feast: An Eight-Session Course for Training Catechists* by Dominic F. Ashkar, PhD, © 1997 Resource Publications, Inc. All rights reserved.

Session 5

Worksheet 2

My Community Reflects Me

I am your (church, community, family…). Make of me what you will; I shall reflect you as clearly as a mirror. If outwardly my appearance is pleasing and inviting, it is because you have made me so. If within my spiritual atmosphere is kindly, yet earnest; reverent, yet friendly; worshipful, yet sympathetic; divine, yet humanly expressed, it is but the manifestation of the spirit of those who constitute my membership.

But if you should, by chance, find me a bit cold or dull, I beg of you not to condemn me, for I imitate the kind of life I receive from you. Of this you may always be assured; I will respond instantly to your every wish practically expressed, for I reflect the image of your own soul. Make of me what you will.

— Anonymous

Session 5

Worksheet 2 (*continued*)

Helpful Guiding Activity

- What image do you reflect? Since your community is a reflection of yourself, take a few moments to rewrite the above passage with additions or changes that will relate to your personal life. It will be for you to keep.

Suggested Reading for Our Next Session
(from *Road to Emmaus: A New Model for Catechesis*)

- "Jesus Said to Them, "O Foolish Ones!", pages 89-92

Session 6

The Catechist and the New Wine

Step 1:
Opening Prayer

Lord Jesus Christ, you are the creator and sustainer of the world. Through you, O Word of God, all things have come into being. You desired to dwell among us and to make us holy through your divinity. The earth and all its inhabitants and all that is in it have been blessed by you. At the wedding at Cana, you accepted the invitation to the feast and there you worked your first miraculous sign, giving the guests special wine as a symbol of your special and genuine love for us. May your wine revive in our hearts your love for us and reveal more clearly your plan for us. Amen.

(You may formulate your own prayer or add to this one:)

Step 2:
Introductory Remarks

(Share the following story:)

A well-known sculptor had a burning ambition to create the greatest statue of Jesus Christ ever made. He began in his oceanside studio by shaping a clay model of a triumphant, regal figure. The head was thrown back and the arms were upraised in a gesture of great majesty. It was his conception of how Christ would look, strong and dominant.

"This will be my masterpiece," he said on the day the clay model was completed. During the night, however, heavy fog rolled into the area and sea spray seeped through a partly opened window. The moisture affected the shape of the clay so that when the artist returned to the studio in the morning, he was shocked at what he found.

Droplets of moisture had formed on the model, creating an illusion of bleeding. The head had dropped. The facial expression had been transformed from one of severity to one of compassion. And the arms had dropped into a posture of welcome. It had become a wounded Christ-figure.

Session 6: The Catechist and the New Wine

The artist stared at the figure, agonizing over the time wasted and the need to begin all over again. Then, inspiration came over him to change his mood. He began to see that this image of Christ was, by far, the truer one. So he carved these words in the base of the newly shaped figure: Come Unto Me.

My friends, we have been reflecting on the Gospel of the wedding at Cana. We will continue our reflection on that passage today as we sit at the feet of the Lord, who constantly invites us saying "Come to me" so that he may reveal his plan of salvation for us and change our lives into new wine that will give the world a fresh new taste.

**Step 3:
Distribute Worksheet 1**

(Before making copies for distribution, see if you wish to add any questions or remarks to it. Preferably before you distribute it, proclaim the Gospel or designate someone else to do so. Following this, give directives and introduce the questions to be discussed in groups for about twenty minutes.)

**Step 4:
Results of
Group Discussion**

(A summary of the main results of the discussion could be written on the board or large sheets of paper so participants may visualize the results and be enriched by the findings of other groups. After this summary, move to the next step, which is the most important part of the session: the presentation of points the participants might have overlooked.)

**Step 5:
General Presentation**

♦ In reading this Gospel text, we cannot find the reason for the lack of wine. We can only speculate. Were the people poor? Did they have more guests than they expected? Or was it a simple lack of foresight?

♦ No matter what the reason for the lack of wine, what might have been an occasion of shame and embarrassment for the married couple and their guests was transformed through the enigmatic relationship among Mary, Jesus, and the servants.

♦ The wine at Cana is not of this earth. Its origin is heaven. The host is not aware of this heavenly origin, but the servants are. Are we ourselves not among those servants of the Word who know the divine origin and that the true New Wine becomes the blood of the New Covenant?

♦ Origen (†254) commented: "Before the Incarnation and the Gospel, the Law was like water, but the intervention of Jesus changed it into inebriating wine." Later on, St. Cyril (†444) said: "Jesus came to sanctify marriage. The Law did not attain perfection but wine did. The Letter kills, but the Spirit gives life."

♦ St. Ambrosius (†397), St. Augustine (†430), and their followers frequently used the mysteries/sacraments as catechetical instruments. Augustine focused on the miracle of Cana as a sign, seeing the coming of Jesus as bringing *newness* and power to the Old Law.

- Theodore of Mopsuestia (†428) said that the response of Jesus to Mary, "My hour has not come," was not denial but an expression of power, which Mary understood and thus had the confidence to approach the servants.

- St. Ephrem (†373) drew a psychological analysis, explaining that in Mary's notice of the lack of wine, she realized there was a reason why she and her son had come to the wedding. St. Ephrem juxtaposed Jesus' miracle of the wine to his later miracle of the multiplication of the bread, finding in these two events a common eucharistic theme in which the life-giving Spirit is communicated to humanity.

- Ephrem's presentation is appealing: Jesus not only gives people bread and wine but also goes on to feed them with his body and blood. Bread and wine give pleasure to the mouth, but the body and blood give salvation to the soul. So the excellent wine Jesus made represents the treasures hidden in his life-giving blood. In this, his first sign, the wine brings joy to the invited guests, but his blood will bring joy to all nations.

- The members of the Christian community are like the guests at the wedding at Cana, drinking the miraculous wine without knowing of the miracle that displayed Jesus' divine power.

- In the event at Cana, water is changed into wine. It is a mystery. So too the liturgy is a mystery that will bring about change in us if we allow it. In fact, the Eucharist can bring about our very divinization. "Holy things for the holy."

- As bearers and teachers of the Word, we are entrusted with this sense of mystery. We are not ourselves the life-giving mystery; our role is, like that of John the Baptizer, the "friend of the groom," to point to the mystery, to take our students to meet Jesus for themselves rather than just talk about him. We see how well John had prepared his followers to become followers of Jesus once they were introduced to him:

  > The next day John was there again with two of his disciples. As he watched Jesus walk by he said, "Look! There is the Lamb of God!" The two disciples heard what he said and followed Jesus. When Jesus turned around and noticed them following him, he asked them, "What are you looking for?" They said to him, "Rabbi (which means Teacher), where do you stay?" "Come and see," he answered. So they went to see where he was lodged, and stayed with him that day. (It was about four in the afternoon).
  >   One of the two who had followed him after hearing John was Simon Peter's brother, Andrew. The first thing he did was seek out his brother Simon and tell him, "We have found the Messiah!" (This term means the Anointed.) He brought him to Jesus, who looked at him and said, "You are Simon, son of John; your name shall be Cephas (which is rendered Peter)."
  >   The next day he wanted to set out for Galilee, but first he came upon Philip. "Follow me," Jesus said to him. Now Philip was from

Session 6: The Catechist and the New Wine

Bethsaida, the same town as Andrew and Peter. Philip sought out Nathanael and told him, "We have found the one Moses spoke of in the law—the prophets too—Jesus, son of Joseph, from Nazareth." Nathanael's response to that was, "Can anything good come from Nazareth?" and Philip replied, "Come, see for yourself." When Jesus saw Nathanael coming toward him, he remarked: "This man is a true Israelite. There is no guile in him." "How do you know me?" Nathanael asked him. "Before Philip called you," Jesus answered, "I saw you under the fig tree." "Rabbi," said Nathanael, "you are the Son of God; you are the king of Israel." Jesus responded: "Do you believe just because I told you I saw you under the fig tree? You will see much greater things than that" (Jn 1:35-50).

- All the disciples in this story, as well as John the Baptizer, were from the Old Law (the simple water) that would be changed into new wine. Can you identify with any of those in the story?

- When John the Baptizer sees Jesus, he presents him. He wants others to follow him. He has trained his beloved disciples so that he can bring them to Christ, not keep them for himself. As disciples, as catechists, we are not the end but the fleeting means. We stand with the servants at the wedding at Cana who know the divine origin of the wine.

- As John's disciples, Andrew and the others in the above Gospel passage hoped for the Messiah. They did not recognize Jesus by themselves. They needed the help of John. We too need the help of someone like him to point out Christ to us. This Jesus is alive in the Gospel, in the church, in the poor, in our students or families, but very often he goes by without our recognition. This is why we need someone to point him out to us. These two disciples, upon seeing him at last, could have merely remarked, "Oh, so that's Jesus," and stayed with John. But because John has prepared them, they make an effort to go find out more about Jesus.

- Jesus asks them, "What are you looking for?" He asks us the same question posed a little differently: "Who and why are you serving?" Plain, everyday water doesn't satisfy the thirst of either the disciples or ourselves. When John's disciples met him that day, they stayed with him. Don't we feel the need to do the same?

- Andrew cannot keep the good news to himself. He goes and tells his brother Simon, "We have found the Messiah." He shares his joy with his brother. He brings him to Jesus, who looks at him with love and compassion and gives him a new name: Peter. Peter would be changed from plain, everyday water into new wine with a new name and a new vocation.

- Like all disciples, Philip does not know the full extent of what discipleship entails because the Lord reveals the meaning of our vocation as we journey, step by step. Philip's initial step in following Jesus is to bring his friend Nathanael to share his own joy of the good news. But Nathanael's first reaction is to comment, "Can anything good come from Nazareth?"

because people in those days held the province of Galilee in low regard. Nathanael overcomes his concern, though, when Jesus comments, "I saw you under the fig tree." This causes Nathanael to exclaim, "How do you know me?" Jesus' answer immediately wins Nathanael's belief.

♦ Jesus' mission is to accomplish the will of the Father. Jesus knows us. He sees us as he did Nathaniel, under our own fig trees. He calls each of us in a special way, always to reveal greater things to us. Are we willing to allow him to change us into the new wine that will bring joy to the hearts of others as well as to our own?

Step 6: Distribute Worksheet 2

(After distributing this worksheet, read or select someone else to read the passage, "Take a Moment to Listen." After this, read the remarks on the worksheet. Mention the suggested readings for the next session.)

Step 7: Sharing and Concluding

♦ Would you like to share any of your reflections or changes you made on your last worksheet?

♦ Before we close our session with a prayer, I wish to remind you to read the suggested passages. As you read them, keep in mind that Jesus is always trying to change our lives of plain, everyday water into new wine of the best vintage.

Step 8: Closing Prayer

Lord Jesus, we thank you for choosing us to be your servants who know what happened to the old water. We thank you for revealing to us the divine origin of this wine and for changing us as you changed the water into wine. We beg you, O Lord, and we beseech your loving heart to forgive our folly and to remove pride from our own hearts. Create in us a new heart that can rejoice in the taste of the new wine. Remove from our eyes the veil of vanity. May your holy body and life-giving blood be the strength that will prepare and lead us to your heavenly banquet. Amen.

(You may formulate your own prayer or add to this one:)

Session 6

Worksheet 1

The Wedding at Cana

On the third day there was a wedding at Cana in Galilee, and the mother of Jesus was there. Jesus and his disciples had likewise been invited to the celebration. At a certain point the wine ran out, and Jesus' mother told him, "They have no more wine." Jesus replied, "Woman, how does this concern of yours involve me? My hour has not yet come." His mother instructed those waiting on table, "Do whatever he tells you." As prescribed for Jewish ceremonial washings, there were at hand six stone water jars, each one holding fifteen to twenty-five gallons. "Fill those jars with water," Jesus ordered, at which they filled them to the brim. "Now," he said, "draw some out and take it to the waiter in charge." They did as he instructed them. THE WAITER IN CHARGE TASTED THE WATER MADE WINE, without knowing where it had come from; only the waiters knew, since they had drawn the water. THEN THE WAITER IN CHARGE CALLED THE GROOM OVER AND REMARKED TO HIM: "PEOPLE USUALLY SERVE THE CHOICE WINE FIRST; THEN WHEN THE GUESTS HAVE BEEN DRINKING AWHILE, A LESSER VINTAGE. WHAT YOU HAVE DONE IS KEEP THE CHOICE WINE UNTIL NOW." Jesus performed this first of his signs at Cana in Galilee. Thus did he reveal his glory, and his disciples believed in him (Jn 2:1-11).

Remarks

- Notice that this time the references to wine are in all capital letters.

- Using the questions on the back of this page, take twenty minutes in small groups to reflect on this passage.

This worksheet was taken from *Come to the Wedding Feast: An Eight-Session Course for Training Catechists* by Dominic F. Ashkar, PhD, © 1997 Resource Publications, Inc. All rights reserved.

Session 6

Worksheet 1 (*continued*)

Helpful Guiding Questions

- What do you think accounted for the wine shortage?

- What was the effect of the lack of wine?

- Did the guests know about the new wine?

- Is there a difference between the water and wine at the wedding?

- Can you see how John the Baptizer and Jesus' disciples were "people of the old water" in their preparation of the way for Jesus? (See Jn 1:35-50.)

- Was Jesus ready to accomplish the Father's plan of salvation and change them from old, everyday water into new wine?

This worksheet was taken from *Come to the Wedding Feast: An Eight-Session Course for Training Catechists* by Dominic F. Ashkar, PhD, © 1997 Resource Publications, Inc. All rights reserved.

Session 6

Worksheet 2

Take a Moment to Listen

Take a moment to listen today
   To what your children are trying to say;
Listen today, whatever you do
   Or they won't be there to listen to you.
Listen to their problems, listen to their needs,
   Praise their smallest triumphs,
   praise their smallest deeds;
Tolerate their chatter, amplify their laughter,
   Find out what's the matter, find out what they're after.
But tell them that you love them, every single night
   And though you scold them, be sure you hold them;
Tell them "Everything's all right;
   tomorrow's looking bright!"
Take a moment to listen today
   To what your children are trying to say;
Listen today, whatever you do
   And they will come back to listen to you.
   — Anonymous

Remarks

- Christ calls us to "come to him" so that we may learn to listen to him, allowing him to change the old water into new wine.

- To be able to listen to Jesus, we need to learn how to listen to little ones.

This worksheet was taken from *Come to the Wedding Feast: An Eight-Session Course for Training Catechists* by Dominic F. Ashkar, PhD, © 1997 Resource Publications, Inc. All rights reserved.

Session 6

Worksheet 2 (*continued*)

Helpful Guiding Activity

- What does this poem bring to mind? Take time to write your own story about listening. It will be for you to keep.

Suggested Readings for Our Next Session
(from *Road to Emmaus: A New Model for Catechesis*)

- "Jesus Walked Along with Them," pages 79-81

- "Jesus Asked the Disciples a Question," pages 83-88

This worksheet was taken from *Come to the Wedding Feast: An Eight-Session Course for Training Catechists* by Dominic F. Ashkar, PhD, © 1997 Resource Publications, Inc. All rights reserved.

Session 7

The Catechist and the Wedding Feast

Step 1:
Opening Prayer

O compassionate Lord, we glorify you, for in the fullness of time you visited your people, and as one of them you participated in their joys such as the wedding at Cana. There you changed water into wine, allowing your mortal creatures to drink of the beverage of eternal life. We ask you, O Lord, to purify us from every sin so that we may taste your mysteries. As through the intercession of your Mother Mary you changed the water into wine, we ask you to change our evil acts into good. Help us open our eyes to your light and delight at the wedding feast like the guests at Cana, with the hope that our faith will be deepened like that of the disciples. Amen.

(You may formulate your own prayer or add to this one:)

Step 2:
Introductory Remarks

(Share the following story:)

A fable is told about a lion and a tiger, who, both thirsty, arrived at a water hole at the same time. Immediately they began to argue about which of them should satisfy its thirst first. The argument became heated. Each animal decided it would rather die than give up the privilege of being first to quench its thirst.

Stubbornly they confronted each other, and their emotions turned to rage. However, their vicious attacks on each other were suddenly interrupted. Looking up toward the sky, they saw circling overhead a flock of vultures waiting for the loser to fall. Quietly, the two beasts turned away from each other and withdrew back into the forest. The thought of being devoured was all they needed to end their quarrel.

Isn't this our own story? Who of us here today does not have a heavy heart because of some problem: perhaps sickness, perhaps many demands, perhaps lack of love? Each of us comes with a heavy cross but also with hope of resurrection. Haven't we, like the animals at the water hole, been involved in dispute? Haven't we all been struggling against ourselves with habits that dominate us or against others trying to be the first to get to the thirst-quenching water? Aren't we all aware of the vultures awaiting our fall to devour us? Don't we all desire a haven where we can celebrate in peace and happiness?

Let us reflect once more on the wedding feast at Cana and reflect on the happiness of the wedding celebration.

Step 3:
Distribute Worksheet 1

(Before making copies for distribution, see if you wish to add any questions or remarks to it. Preferably before you distribute it, proclaim the Gospel or designate someone else to do so. Following this, give directives and introduce the questions to be discussed in groups for about twenty minutes.)

Step 4:
Results of Group Discussion

(A summary of the main results of the discussion could be written on the board or large sheets of paper so that participants may visualize the results and be enriched by the findings of other groups. After this summary, move to the next step, which is the most important part of the session: presentation of points the participants might have overlooked.)

Step 5:
General Presentation

- In the Cana event we find two particularly clear aspects: human love and a window opening onto the great mystery of the wedding feast of God and humanity.

- We see God, who becomes more than a friend to the humans he created in his desire for close union with us through his son Jesus Christ. God is always in search of his people. He draws closer and engages in dialogue with us. We become like two persons in love. As we read in the Old Testament, from the beginning of Christianity the church has been portrayed in bridal imagery in covenant relationship, including:

    Love: "I will take you as my own people, and you shall have me as your God" (Ex 6:7).

    Jealousy: "For I the LORD, your God, am a jealous God…" (Ex 20:5).

- God becomes a personal God who loves, but still he must compete with other gods in which the people of Babylonia, Canaan, and Egypt believed.

- While these gods are engaged in marriage with humans or even with the earth itself through fertility rites, the one true God remains unique. He engages in a covenant with his people, as the prophets constantly reminded the people. Hosea, for instance, writes: "When Israel was a child I loved him, out of Egypt I called my son" (11:1). The prophets awaken the people's consciousness, clarifying this covenant as God's marriage with his people.

- Throughout the reign of kings in Israel, this love is often broken, for worship of pagan gods is mixed with worship of the unique, personal God. The prophet Hosea expresses the brokenness of his heart because of the adulterous spouse (1:2-8). Adultery, like prostitution, reflects lack of fidelity, love, and gratitude. The only remedy is to return to the true love. To return is to convert, to avoid judgment, and to open to a new love because God never ceases loving. This new love, this New Covenant, will be unbroken because it is eternal.

- The prophet Jeremiah sees the broken covenant as an "affair of the heart," a refusal of repentance that leads to the aggravation and increase of sin, making the spouse not only an adulterer but also a prostitute. (Jerusalem did not learn from the experience of Samaria [Jer 3:6-12].) A new heart, a new covenant, and a new conversion are needed, but this time, it is the spouse who must search for God.

- The prophet Ezekiel expresses covenant marriage in an allegorical way, comparing two sisters, Jerusalem and Samaria, as daughters of the same pagan mother, one of which profits from its sinful experience and seeks pardon and purification, even though imperfectly.

- Punishment and a period of lamentation come to the adulterous spouse. Only God can save this desolate spouse, who returns in tears and prayers, converted.

- With the Exile comes the time for new betrothal. Punishment comes to an end. God comes to ransom his spouse, who wakes from drunkenness, hoping to rediscover her dignity and beauty (Is 51:17).

- Now at last God's saving love can break through. Even if a mother forgets her child, God will not forget Israel. This saving love of his is eternal, making the heart of his bride rejoice and forget her past. It is time to give birth to a new people. The rejected, chastised spouse recovers her dignity and beauty.

- We find three main features in this spousal imagery of the Old Testament prophets that will continue to be developed in the New Testament:

    1. God's patient and forgiving love
    2. sin as the refusal of God's loving plan
    3. the new hope that salvation brings in the nuptials of Christ with his church

- All are invited to this wedding feast. Yet even if we are saved, we fear we might be among the rejected. We need to be ready. We have been purified by baptism and nourished by the Eucharist, our food in our journey, so that when the day comes we will be able to meet him.

- In the Old Testament God was seen as loving but primarily all-powerful. In the New Testament, however, God manifests his power through the generosity of his love.

Session 7: The Catechist and the Wedding Feast

- God engages humanity in a wedding feast, a union of love of which Christ is the living proof. The church exists in an atmosphere of a wedding feast in which Christ's disciples enjoy the love that never dies.

- To be part of that eternal wedding feast, we must be like little children, as we see in the following two Gospel passages:

  > People were bringing their little children to him to have him touch them, but the disciples were scolding them for this. Jesus became indignant when he noticed it and said to them: "Let the children come to me and do not hinder them. It is to just such as these that the kingdom of God belongs. I assure you that whoever does not accept the reign of God like a little child shall not take part in it." Then he embraced them and blessed them, placing his hands on them (Mk 10:13-16).

  > Just then the disciples came up to Jesus with the question, "Who is of greatest importance in the kingdom of God?" He called a little child over and stood him in their midst and said: "I assure you, unless you change and become like little children you will not enter the kingdom of God. Whoever makes himself lowly, becoming like this child, is of greatest importance in that heavenly reign" (Mt 18:1-4).

- What do these Gospel texts have to do with the story of the eternal wedding celebration? Let us reflect for a moment on these texts.

- Imagine mothers coming from afar, bringing their children to be blessed by Jesus. Later on, they would proudly remind their children of this event, like the happy parents of children whom the pope touches, blesses, or holds. The parents in the Gospel stories come with enthusiasm but find their children prevented from approaching Jesus. For the disciples as well as other adults, these children are merely a nuisance.

- Jesus' reaction is quite different. "Let them come to me." For him they are fully human. "He embraced them and blessed them, placing his hands on them." Jesus' goodness reflects the goodness of God the Father. Through this attitude, Jesus invites his disciples to think about the kingdom in a new way. There is a condition to gain this kingdom: it is forbidden to become old! To become old is to become independent and self-absorbed and perhaps to assume that faith is mainly for children.

- Jesus knows that the little ones are not perfect, but he sees in them the purity of heart and innocence that we are invited to regain. To make this point, Jesus brings forward a child and sets him in the midst of the crowd.

- Jesus does not invite us to become childish but childlike. The doctrine of the Gospel is not for children but for the mature. Yet to be a child is to be dependent on parents, and Jesus invites us to have this filial attitude toward God the Father. To be childlike is to accept not being master of our lives, not making our own rules and laws. To be childlike means to recognize God as Father. Jesus himself is a perfect example. Although he did not stay a little child, or childish, he remained a son with a filial attitude toward his Father, glorifying him.

- To be childlike does not mean to stop growing or to go backward. To be childlike involves growth, maturity, and progress. It brings a new life: "No one can enter into God's kingdom without being begotten of water and Spirit" (Jn 3:5). Jesus invites us to enter into a new world where, like him, we become servants. Only the son can become heir. We do not enter this kingdom by right, but we need to become like little children spiritually. To do so is not to return to the past but to look to the future. To do so does not mean that we overcome the malice of this world but that we gain the kingdom. We cannot gain this kingdom if we do not become "epiclesis people," as St. Paul says: "All who are led by the Spirit of God are sons of God" (Rom 8:14). The term "epiclesis people" refers to those who are led by the Holy Spirit, who brings all God's children to the eternal wedding celebration.

Step 6:
Distribute Worksheet 2

(After distributing this worksheet, read or select someone else to read the story, "End of Night and Beginning of Day." After this, read the remarks on the worksheet. Mention the suggested readings for the next session.)

Step 7:
Sharing and Concluding

- Would you like to share any of your reflections or notes you made on your last worksheet?

- Before we close our session with a prayer, I wish to remind you to read the suggested passages. As you read them, keep in mind that we are all invited to share in the celebration of the eternal wedding feast and that to do so we must live as children of light.

Step 8:
Closing Prayer

O Lord, you work wonders in our midst. At the wedding at Cana, you performed your first sign and changed water into excellent wine to help the guests celebrate. Quench the thirst of our hearts, O Lord, with the wine of your divine love. May our actions prepare us to be your disciples on the journey to your eternal heavenly wedding banquet to which you, the Bridegroom, call us all. Help us exchange our mortality for your divinity. Amen.

(You may formulate your own prayer or add to this one:)

Session 7

Worksheet 1

The Wedding at Cana

On the third day there was a WEDDING at Cana in Galilee, and the mother of Jesus was there. Jesus and his disciples had likewise been invited to the CELEBRATION. At a certain point the wine ran out, and Jesus' mother told him, "They have no more wine." Jesus replied, "Woman, how does this concern of yours involve me? My hour has not yet come." His mother instructed those waiting on table, "Do whatever he tells you." As prescribed for Jewish ceremonial washings, there were at hand six stone water jars, each one holding fifteen to twenty-five gallons. "Fill those jars with water," Jesus ordered, at which they filled them to the brim. "Now," he said, "draw some out and take it to the waiter in charge." They did as he instructed them. The waiter in charge tasted the water made wine, without knowing where it had come from; only the waiters knew, since they had drawn the water. Then the waiter in charge called the groom over and remarked to him: "People usually serve the choice wine first; then when the GUESTS have been drinking awhile, a lesser vintage. What you have done is keep the choice wine until now." Jesus performed this first of his signs at Cana in Galilee. Thus did he reveal his glory, and his disciples believed in him (Jn 2:1-11).

Remarks

- Notice that this time the words pertaining to the wedding celebration are in all capital letters.

- Using the quesions on the back of this page, take twenty minutes in small groups to reflect on this Gospel passage.

This worksheet was taken from *Come to the Wedding Feast: An Eight-Session Course for Training Catechists* by Dominic F. Ashkar, PhD, © 1997 Resource Publications, Inc. All rights reserved.

Session 7

Worksheet 1 (*continued*)

Helpful Guiding Questions

- What are the most important characteristics of a wedding feast or celebration?

- What could destroy the joy of a wedding celebration?

- What makes a wedding feast celebration continue throughout a marriage?

- What could make a wedding celebration cease to exist at some point in married life?

- Is there any connection between the wedding feast celebration and the kingdom of God?

- What is (are) the main condition(s) to being part of this kingdom of God? (See Mk 10:15-16 and Mt 18:1-4.)

Session 7

Worksheet 2

End of Night and Beginning of Day

Late one night the Teacher sat around a blazing fire with a small number of disciples. Their conversation was broken by periods of silence when they gazed at the stars or stared into the glowing embers. Suddenly the Teacher posed a question: "How can we know when the night has ended and the day has begun?"

Eagerly a young man answered, "You know the night is over when you can look off in the distance and tell which animal is a dog and which is a sheep. Is that the right answer, Teacher?"

"It is a good answer," the Teacher said, "but not quite the answer I would give."

A second disciple ventured a guess. "You know the night is over when the light falls on the leaves and you can tell whether it is an olive tree or a fig tree," he said.

Once again the Teacher shook his head. "That was a fine answer. Still, it is not the answer I seek," he said gently.

Immediately the disciples began to argue with one another. Finally, one of them begged, "Answer your question, Teacher, for we cannot think of another response."

The Teacher looked intently at the eager faces before he spoke. "When you look into the eyes of another human being and see a brother or a sister, you will know it is morning. If you cannot see a brother or a sister, you will know that, no matter what time it is, for you it will always be night and you will be in the dark."

Remarks

- We are all called to be part of the celebration of the wedding feast.

- To be part of the feast, we must be children of light and live as brothers and sisters.

This worksheet was taken from *Come to the Wedding Feast: An Eight-Session Course for Training Catechists* by Dominic F. Ashkar, PhD, © 1997 Resource Publications, Inc. All rights reserved.

Session 7

Worksheet 2 (continued)

Helpful Guiding Activity

- Relate some episodes in your own life in which you did not "know when the night ended and the day began." This will be for you to keep.

Suggested Readings for Our Next Session
(from *Road to Emmaus: A New Model for Catechesis*)

- "Jesus Made As If to Go Further," pages 93-96

- "He Took Bread, Blessed, Broke and Distributed It," pages 97-103

Session 8

The Catechist and Prayer

**Step 1:
Opening Prayer**

Lord God, you continue to call righteous guests to your spiritual banquet, which is a free gift from you. You continue to invite us, your faithful children, to your kingdom. As you took on our humanity to make us sharers in your divinity, so we ask you to continue to enrich us with the abundance of your heavenly gifts and divine wisdom. Like your Mother Mary, may we have a deep faith and prayer life so that when we ask, we can be sure that our prayer will always be heard. We also ask you to continue giving us your "wine pressed out on the cross," quenching our thirst with love and compassion and washing our sins so that with pure hearts we may always share in your holy banquet feast. Amen.

(You may formulate your own prayer or add to this one:)

**Step 2:
Introductory Remarks**

(Share the following story:)

A story is told about an oilman who started to drill a new well on his land, but after drilling a deep hole found no oil. The owner decided that it was a dead hole and told the crew boss to cap the well. He would write it off as a complete loss.

Meanwhile, the foreman called to the driller and asked how much "rope" was left on the rig. In oil-field jargon, "rope" refers to the drilling pipe. "About six to eight feet," replied the driller. "Then keep on drilling deeper," shouted the foreman.

After drilling only two feet more, the men struck oil. This well became one of the most productive in the entire oil field.

We can learn a lot about life from this story. While there is still "rope," there is still room for hope.

We can also learn a lot from this story about our spiritual life and the life of the Spirit in us. Spiritually, when we look at our own efforts and achievements, we feel like stopping the drilling and writing off our loss. But in this temptation, we forget who we are. We forget the life of the Holy Spirit within us. So if you are experiencing some difficulties in teaching and have considered quitting, know that there is still "rope." We need to pray about such a vocation and such a decision. For this reason our last topic will be "the catechist and prayer." Once again, we look at the Gospel of the wedding at Cana.

Step 3:
Distribute Worksheet 1

(Before making copies for distribution, see if you wish to add any questions or remarks to it. Preferably before you distribute it, proclaim the Gospel or designate someone else to do so. Following this, give directive and introduce the questions to be discussed in groups for about twenty minutes.)

Step 4:
Results of
Group Discussion

(A summary of the main results of the discussion could be written on the board or large sheets of paper so that participants may visualize the results and be enriched by the findings of other groups. After this, move to the next step, which is the most important part of the session: presentation of points the participants might have overlooked.)

Step 5:
General Presentation

◆ My friends, very often we all forget that we are, like Mary, filled with the Holy Spirit. Yes, we are "epiclesis people." What does it mean to be "epiclesis people"? The epiclesis is the "calling down upon" or the "invocation" of the Holy Spirit. The epiclesis is that part of the divine liturgy when the priest calls upon the Holy Spirit to descend and overshadow the offering, making it, the bread, the body of Christ and the mixture of the cup, the blood of Christ. Indeed, it is the Holy Spirit who is the source, the beginning and the end of all things.

◆ Are you wondering what this has to do with Mary or with our topic? Mary is our model of what it means to be an "epiclesis people." She knows how to persevere, how to go deeper and deeper in her faith. Like the persistent foreman, she knows that, while there is still "rope," there is also still room for hope.

◆ Mary conceives Jesus by the power of the Holy Spirit, even though she does not totally understand the full meaning of the mystery. It is the Holy Spirit that makes her a "servant of God," as he does us. As servants of God, we are a kingdom of priests. It is the Holy Spirit that takes her to visit her cousin Elizabeth, where John is sanctified in the womb. It is the Holy Spirit who inspires her to express a prayer to Jesus at the wedding at Cana, and her prayer, her request, changes God's plan even though his hour has not come.

◆ It is through the Holy Spirit that Mary, who is first of all the Mother of Jesus, becomes the woman at the foot of the cross (Jn 2:4; 19:26), the New Eve and Mother of the whole Christ, the church. On Pentecost morning, in Mary's presence, this same Holy Spirit brings forth in a virginal way the body of Christ comprised of ourselves, the church.

- The church manifests the Spirit of Christ in a new community of men and women called to be divinized. The liturgy we celebrate becomes the source of our divinization and our becoming "epiclesis people." For Mary as for us all, it is the Spirit that changes our hearts so that they can persevere in the hope of deepening and changing, of divinizing our whole being. This is how we become "epiclesis people" invited to accept our mission of becoming servants of the Spirit, divinizing and purifying the world around us.

- Deepening and witnessing to our faith cannot be improvised. It requires compassion like Mary's, always new. She is our model of faith, hope, and charity. Witnessing, responding to the Spirit's inspiration, becoming "epiclesis people," leads to the eternal celebration in heaven.

- St. Ephrem claims that Jesus' answer to Mary at the wedding at Cana was so that people would see the necessity of prayer. Others see in Jesus' response a reminder to his mother of the separation that is to take place between them as he begins his public life. No matter what the reason for his response, we must agree with Ephrem on the necessity of prayer. After Jesus' response, Mary becomes more persistent in her prayer as she asks the servants to do whatever he tells them. Mary does not interfere in her son's mission but makes it known that she relies on his intervention. How often do people give up after what they call "unanswered prayer"?

- Mary's perseverance is successful and Jesus' first miracle occurs. This miracle of Jesus, who had said at the time of Mary's request that his hour had not yet come, reflects the power of prayer. "Ask and you shall receive."

- Thus our prayers can influence divine action. In the same region where Jesus' first miracle occurred, we find yet another example of this in the story of the Canaanite woman, who, like Mary, brought about Jesus' help by being persistent in asking (Mt 15:24).

- Do we remember to pray for those we lead and teach?

Step 6:
Distribute Worksheet 2

(Before distributing this worksheet, tell the story of "The Vision of the Snail." Then distribute the worksheet. Tell your audience that you are going to leave them with this wise vision, even though what we want may seem to come slowly or seem impossible to get.)

Step 7:
Sharing and Concluding

- Would you like to share any of your reflections regarding our program?

- Before we close with a prayer, I would like to express my sincerest thanks for all you have done as servants of the Word of God. Since our last talk was about prayer, I would like to leave you with the following words:

How to Worship

Be silent.
Be thoughtful.
Be reverent, for this is the House of God.
Before the service, speak to God.
During the service, let God speak to you.
After the service, speak to one another.

Step 8: Closing Prayer

We ask you, O Lord, always to accept us at the banquet table of your kingdom, allowing us to drink your new wine as we journey toward your eternal wedding feast. As you gave joy to the guests at the wedding at Cana by changing the water into wine, give us, through our prayer life, a taste of the joy that awaits us in your heavenly kingdom. Help us through our prayer life to become servants, thankful because they know of the mystery of your first sign, which was only the beginning of still more signs that continue to be manifested in and through us. Blessed are we because "happy are those who have been invited to the wedding feast of the Lamb" (Rev 19:9).

(You may formulate your own prayer or add to this one:)

Session 8

Worksheet 1

The Wedding at Cana

On the third day there was a wedding at Cana in Galilee, and the mother of Jesus was there. Jesus and his disciples had likewise been invited to the celebration. At a certain point the wine ran out, and JESUS' MOTHER TOLD HIM, "THEY HAVE NO MORE WINE." JESUS REPLIED, "WOMAN, HOW DOES THIS CONCERN OF YOURS INVOLVE ME? MY HOUR HAS NOT YET COME." HIS MOTHER INSTRUCTED THOSE WAITING ON TABLE, "DO WHATEVER HE TELLS YOU." As prescribed for Jewish ceremonial washings, there were at hand six stone water jars, each one holding fifteen to twenty-five gallons. "Fill those jars with water," Jesus ordered, at which they filled them to the brim. "Now," he said, "draw some out and take it to the waiter in charge." They did as he instructed them. The waiter in charge tasted the water made wine, without knowing where it had come from; only the waiters knew, since they had drawn the water. Then the waiter in charge called the groom over and remarked to him: "People usually serve the choice wine first; then when the guests have been drinking awhile, a lesser vintage. What you have done is keep the choice wine until now." Jesus performed this first of his signs at Cana in Galilee. Thus did he reveal his glory, and his disciples believed in him (Jn 2:1-11).

Remarks

- Notice that this time Mary's prayer is in all capital letters.

- Using the questions on the back of this page, take twenty minutes in small groups to reflect on this Gospel passage.

This worksheet was taken from *Come to the Wedding Feast: An Eight-Session Course for Training Catechists* by Dominic F. Ashkar, PhD, © 1997 Resource Publications, Inc. All rights reserved.

Session 8

Worksheet 1 (continued)

Helpful Guiding Questions

- How much importance do you—especially as a religious educator—give to prayer in your daily life?

- What connection do you see between prayer and the Holy Spirit?

- What connection is there between Mary's prayer life and the Holy Spirit?

- How was Mary's life affected and filled by the Holy Spirit?

- What is the Holy Spirit's role in the life of us all, first as individuals and then as a community?

- What is the importance of perseverance in prayer?

- Is there any connection between prayer and the divine plan or action?

- Do you personally find that prayer has power?

This worksheet was taken from *Come to the Wedding Feast: An Eight-Session Course for Training Catechists* by Dominic F. Ashkar, PhD, © 1997 Resource Publications, Inc. All rights reserved.

Session 8

Worksheet 2

The Vision of the Snail

One raw, windy day in spring, a snail started to climb a cherry tree. Some birds in a nearby tree sniped their ridicule. "Hey, you dumb snail," squawked one of them, "where do you think you're going?" "Why are you climbing that tree?" others chimed in. "There are no cherries on it."

"There will be some by the time I get there," replied the snail.

Remarks

- The snail had a vision the birds did not have.

This worksheet was taken from *Come to the Wedding Feast: An Eight-Session Course for Training Catechists* by Dominic F. Ashkar, PhD, © 1997 Resource Publications, Inc. All rights reserved.

Session 8

Worksheet 2 (*continued*)

Helpful Guiding Activity

- This story might help us understand the meaning of perseverance in prayer. Take courage and think of what you are going to do in the coming year and how you might prepare for it.

Suggested Reading
(from *Road to Emmaus: A New Model for Catechesis*)

- "They Got Up Immediately and Returned to Jerusalem," pages 111-115

- Try to read all of *Road to Emmaus* during the coming months.

Conclusion

The Cana event carries a meaning that is much beyond the visible. It announces a renewed world, a world that is transfigured. It is, then, a christological manifestation, an epiphany of the glory of the Son of God. It is abundant wine of superior quality and mysterious origin. Through this first sign of his, Jesus begins to reveal the salvation he brings as the Messiah. This sign is a call to faith. It also shows us:

- Mary's fruitful intercession and powerful prayer

- the symbolism of the heavenly wedding feast

- the eucharistic wine

Cana is the inauguration of the Spirit's readiness to renew the face of the earth by transforming us into "epiclesis people." In following Mary's example, we are led by the Spirit. Cana is thus an occasion for us to build our own future, our own home, which Christ prepared for us and promised us. But what kind of a home are we building? Let the following story speak to you of the need to build well, for if we do not take our vocation seriously, we will be cheating ourselves:

> A young carpenter married a building contractor's daughter. Soon after the wedding, the father-in-law decided to do something to help his new son-in-law in his career.
>
> The father-in-law said: "Son, I don't want you to start your construction business at the bottom the way I did. Go out to my work site and build the best house this town has ever seen. Let it be not only the best house but a show place, and when you finish, turn it over to me."
>
> The son-in-law wanted to make a killing rather than build the best house. He made a deal with a shady wholesaler and installed sub-standard lumber, shingles, cinder blocks, cement, etc., and he billed for the "best" materials. The two cheaters split the profits from their deception. And the son-in-law finally presented his father-in-law with the keys to the newly finished house.
>
> "Is it the best house ever built, as I asked you, with the best materials?" said the father-in-law.
>
> "It sure is," said the son-in-law.
>
> "All right, where's the final bill? And did you include a good profit in it for yourself?"

"Uh, well... Here it is," the son-in-law replied, "and, yes, I did."

"Okay. Let me write out a check. Do you have the deed with you?"

As he accepted the deed, the father-in-law said, "I didn't tell you why I wanted that house to be the best ever built. I wanted it to be something special that I could give to you and my daughter to show you how much I love you. Here, take the deed and the keys. Go live in that show place; it's yours now. Go live in the house you built—for yourself!"

The young man went away, shattered and frustrated. He had thought he was making a fortune at his father-in-law's expense by shaving money here and there with inferior materials and shortcuts, but in the end he had cheated and fooled only himself.

As for us—what kind of house are we building?

Resources for Catechizing Adults

EUCHARIST

An Eight-Session
Ritual-Catechesis Experience for Adults

Susan S. Jorgensen

Paper, 200 pages, 8½" x 11", ISBN: 0-89390-293-4

"Susan Jorgensen has created a living, breathing, working process for community transformation... respectful of differences, open to the variety of approaches, ready to use and well designed, it is a strong resource and strong spark to our ritual imaginations." – Catholic Press Association Book Award Judges

Participants in this eight-week program work through the prayers of the eucharistic liturgy, from opening rite to dismissal, and emerge with deep understanding of the words and gestures of the Eucharist.

TRANSFIGURATION CATECHESIS

A New Vision Based on the Liturgy
and the Catechism of the Catholic Church

Dominic F. Ashkar, PhD

Paper, 192 pages, 5½" x 8½", ISBN: 0-89390-342-6

Does publication of the *Catechism of the Catholic Church* signal a move away from liturgical reform? Not in the eyes of Fr. Dominic F. Ashkar. This religious educator says the Catechism springs from the same well as the Liturgy. In fact, they work together to suggest seven principles that can rejuvenate your catechetical program. These principles, derived from the story of the transfiguration, begin with the call of a disciple to ascend a high mountain and end with the sending of the disciple on a journey.

ROAD TO EMMAUS

A New Model for Catechesis

Dominic F. Ashkar, PhD

Paper, 200 pages, 5½" x 8½", ISBN: 0-89390-266-7

Put new life into your teaching. Study, reflect, integrate the ten principles outlined in this book and the results will be evident in your programs and in parish life. Great for catechist training.

RCIA SPIRITUALITY

Formation for the Catechumenate Team

Barbara Hixon with Reflection Questions by Gael Gensler, OSF

Paper, 192 pages, 5½" x 8½", ISBN: 0-89390-399-X

"Like the RCIA itself, this book is dangerous, scary, risky, an invitation to mayhem and mystery. Don't read it if you want to keep adult initiation and conversion something you do to others and not what God does to you." — Rev. James B. Dunning

Barbara Hixon and Gael Gensler have a straightforward message: the catechumenal process is not something you do to someone else. It's something that happens to you, the team member, as much as to the catechumen. They take you deep into the spirituality of the catechumenate process and show you how each step — from pre-catechumenate to mystagogia — will change your life. Gael Gensler's questions help turn this book, a revision of the original RCIA Ministry, into a useful group formation tool for the catechumenate team.

CATECHIZING WITH LITURGICAL SYMBOLS

25 Hands-on Sessions for Teens and Adults

Pamela J. Edwards

Paper, 128 pages, 8½" x 11", ISBN: 0-89390-401-5

These 25 liturgical symbols will touch you. You know the power of symbols. The power to inspire. To enrich. To deepen faith. But most resources on symbols are dry, wordy, theoretical treatises. Not this one. *Catechizing with Liturgical Symbols* is a practical, 25-session program for expanding family understanding and sensitivity for symbols. In these sessions, people interact with these symbols, are touched by them, and let them become a part of their faith experience. Creating symbols can also be used as therapeutic exercises that promote healing. The examples included in this work can be done at home, in the classroom or with a worship environment, all with a minimum of aesthetic training and only a small investment in time or money.

Call Toll-Free 1-888-273-7782 for current prices.
See last page for ordering information.

More Teaching Resources

PARABLES OF CONVERSION
Homilies and Stories Based on the Lectionary
Lou Ruoff
Paper, 128 pages, 5½" x 8½", ISBN: 0-89390-403-1

"Everyone, it seems, has a favorite Father Lou homily. The one about the Lone Ranger, complete with theme song. The time he brought a sheep to the altar. The one about his buddy in Philly who tattooed his girlfriend Sue's name all over his body and ended up marrying a girl named Sharon." — The Virginian-Pilot and the Ledger-Star

Father Lou is back — this time with stories focused on the conversion experience. To make a point about conversion, look into *Parables of Conversion*. Some are narratives, others more poetic. Some are dialogue, others are reflections that occur only within one's heart of hearts. Some are fantasy, others help you experience what it is like to live in the gutter with the muck of humanity. But each tale relates a set of experiences that lead, through grace, to a moment of conversion. And each parable poses a spiritual question while remaining open-ended — the better to encourage discussion and reflection.

PARABLES OF BELONGING
Discipleship and Commitment in Everyday Life
Lou Ruoff
Paper, 112 pages, 5½" x 8½", ISBN: 0-89390-253-5

The collection of stories in *Parables of Belonging* recognizes the ability of average people to minister to others in their lives just by carrying out their day-to-day activities. Telling these stories will help listeners acknowledge and rejoice in their own "hidden" giftedness and invigorate your community.

WINDOWS INTO THE LECTIONARY
Seasonal Anecdotes for Preaching and Teaching
Donald L. Deffner
Paper, 160 pages, 5½" x 8½", ISBN: 0-89390-393-0

Preachers love a good anecdote, an evocative story, or a short illustration. Too often, they can only find items that fall flat because they a) don't fit the reading, b) don't connect to real life, c) make simplistic analogies, or d) don't have a punchline. No such problem with this collection. Homiletics professor Donald Deffner has made a significant effort to locate short sermon illustrations that work on all levels. This collection packs a punch. The illustrations carry a universal spiritual truth that can be applied to the hearer's personal world. Many stories have a telling climax. All of them are connected to the church year — and there is an index that enables you to search for stories by season, theme, or scripture verse.

SEASONAL ILLUSTRATIONS FOR PREACHING AND TEACHING
Donald L. Deffner
Paper, 176 pages, 5½" x 8½", ISBN: 0-89390-234-9

Preachers and teachers: use these illustrations to get your listeners' attention and enrich their understanding of the church year. These short bits will always make them think.

THE DREAM CATCHER
20 Lectionary-Based Stories for Teaching and Preaching
James L. Henderschedt
Paper, 128 pages, 5½" x 8½", ISBN: 0-89390-339-6

"Clever, poignant, humorous, in touch with our human reality, his stories, once read, are not the end, but rather the beginning of insight into my journey toward a loving God..." — Rev. Edward Miller, pastor, St. Bernardine's Catholic Church

Call Toll-Free 1-888-273-7782 for current prices.
See last page for ordering information.

Lectionary-Based Catechesis

CELEBRATING THE LECTIONARY

Celebrating The Lectionary (CTL) is a Roman Catholic lectionary-based catechetical program for parishes and schools. The program offers teacher packets for six age groups, all coordinated around the same Sunday readings, covering all Sundays from September through June. Additional packets provide for Children's Liturgy of the Word, bilingual family handout masters, a packet for Children's Catechumenate, plus support packets for homilists and DREs.

Here is what you get in every Catechetical Teacher Packet:

Overview of the Year

The overview shows the lesson themes for each Sunday of the year, and also the themes for the Units that the lessons are grouped into.

Unit Background Sheets

These give background information on the season, the scriptural context of the readings, and the connection between the reading and the related doctrine. They also explain how the theme derives from the readings, and give notes for future preparations that need to be made more than one week in advance.

Sunday Background Sheets

These give commentary on the three readings and the psalm, explaining the historical context, the literary context and the liturgical context of each.

Lesson Plans

Each lesson is divided into the following components: Purpose, Preparation, Opening, Introducing the Theme, Closing. Many include several options for each component.

Activity Sheets

Activity Sheets are handouts that you photocopy and give to each student. They eliminate the need for costly, separate student textbooks.

Resource Sheets

These provide additional material needed in specific lessons. They often include stories, meditations, and craft patterns for the catechist. They are not meant to be handed out.

Teaching Pictures

These are pictures to be shown to the children as you tell a story. Because you paint or color them yourself, you can adapt them to the ethnic makeup of your community.

Catechist's Supplement

This is an additional resource provided with each teaching packet. It contains developmental information, skills for effective catechesis, suggestions for preparation, alternate craft ideas, games, activities, etc.

Available Grade Levels:
Nursery (Ages 3-4)
Beginner (Ages 4-6)
Primary (Ages 7-8)
Intermediate (Ages 9-11)
Junior-Senior (Ages 11-15)
Adult (Ages 15 and up)

Annual Purchase
Value Priced
1 packet per teacher
Student material reproduced from teacher's packet.
FREE information booklets available. Packets delivered by: mid-August.

Call Toll-Free 1-888-273-7782 for current prices.
See last page for ordering information.

Children's Lectionary Resources

CHILDREN'S CATECHUMENATE

From CELEBRATING THE LECTIONARY

Edited by Liz Montes

Looseleaf, 312 pages, 8½" x 11", ISBN: 0-89390-427-9
Published annually in August

This new 300-page packet is loaded with resources that catechists have been demanding. This new packet contains everything you need to run an effective catechumenate process for children all year round. It has Sunday Background Sheets commenting on the readings, session plans with plenty of options for older and younger children, and a Parent-Child Sharing Sheet. Like other packets in the CELEBRATING THE LECTIONARY series, this one includes all the materials the catechist needs, including photocopiable masters. This packet makes a great companion for the book, *Children's Catechumenate: A Catechist's Guide.*

CHILDREN'S CATECHUMENATE:

A Catechist's Guide

Philip J. McBrien

Paper, 104 pages, 8½" x 11", ISBN: 0-89390-413-9

Here is a book that focuses on the initiation rites themselves. The first part of the book includes background information on the catechumenate in general, the children's catechumenate in particular, and explanation of current practice on children's catechumenate. The second part of the book includes a set of reproducible handouts for family catechesis on each period or rite. In addition, there are guidelines for doing periodic interviews with the families. This book can be used independently or in conjunction with the CELEBRATING THE LECTIONARY Children's Catechumenate Packet, part of a lectionary-based catechesis program.

Call Toll-Free 1-888-273-7782 for current prices.
See last page for ordering information.

Resources for Working With Youth

YOUTH MINISTRY ACTIVITY BOOK

For Ages 11-14

Rose Thomas Stupak

Paper, 105 pages, 5½" x 8½", ISBN: 0-89390-127-X

"The author offers a cafeteria of ideas that you can build on, according to your own situation. She provides you with the basic ingredients to structure your own pilgrimage, retreat, service project, dramatization, song, and pantomime for your specific group of teens." — Liguorian Magazine.

LOVING OUR NEIGHBOR, THE EARTH

Creation-Spirituality Activities for 9-11 Year Olds

Christie L. Jenkins, PhD

Paper, 125 perforated pages, 8½" x 11", ISBN: 0-89390-204-7

Twenty illustrated and easy-to-follow lesson plans that teach children about environmental issues with a theological as well as a scientific perspective. Includes student activity sheets which can be photocopied.

YOUR WILL BE DONE ON EARTH

Eco-Spirituality Activities for 12-15 Year Olds

Christie L. Jenkins, PhD

Paper, Eighteen lesson plans, 120 pages, 8½" x 11"
ISBN: 0-89390-254-3

"An excellent book for teaching adolescents about environmental issues from a religious, theological, and scientific perspective."— Theological Book Service.

THE SEVEN PRINCIPLES OF EFFECTIVE YOUTH MINISTRY

Mark Springer and Cheryl Smith

Paper 192 pages, 5½" x 8½", ISBN: 0-89390-341-8

"Up to date without being trendy, God-centered without being impossible, the authors are offering us something that is both information and inspiration... this book will feed the passion."—Richard Rohr, OFM Center for Action and Contemplation.

CULTIVATING CHARACTER

Parent-Teacher Resources
for Grades 9, 10, 11, and 12

Richard K. Buchholz

Stapled, illustrated, photocopiable pages, 32 pages, 8½" x 11"
ISBN: 0-89390-407-4 (Grade 9)
ISBN: 0-89390-406-6 (Grade 10)
ISBN: 0-89390-405-8 (Grade 11)
ISBN: 0-89390-404-X (Grade 12)

How do you instill good character in young people? According to Richard Buchholz, you keep it simple. You get teachers and parents to work together. And you use lots of praise. With his Cultivating Character resource books, you use these principles to prepare young people to become good parents, workers, and citizens. Each book contains a "thought for the month" master, along with background information, that can be photocopied and posted on bulletin boards, given to students for hanging in lockers or keeping with their personal journals, and mailed to parents for posting on refrigerator doors. With constant repetition — Buchholtz recommends 20 times a day — the "thought for the month" can have a powerful effect on the behavior of a young person. Simple. Easy. And effective.

Call Toll-Free 1-888-273-7782 for current prices.
See last page for ordering information.

Resources for Story and Drama

STORYTELLING STEP BY STEP
Marsh Cassady, PhD

Paper, 156 pages, 5½" x 8½", ISBN: 0-893890-183-0

Marsh Cassady, a director, actor, and storyteller, shows you all the steps to successful storytelling: selecting the right story for your audience, adapting your story for different occasions, analyzing it so that you can present it well, preparing your audience, and presenting the story. Includes many examples of stories.

CREATIVE STORYTELLING
Marsh Cassady, PhD

Three Audio Cassettes

These audio cassettes are adapted from the author's books *Storytelling Step By Step* and *Creating Stories for Storytelling*. Learn all the steps to successful storytelling: selecting the right story for your audience, adapting your story for different occasions and audiences, analyzing it, preparing your audience, and presenting the story. You'll also find ideas for creating your own original stories, plotting a story, creating tension, and writing dialogue that will keep your listeners on the edge of their chairs. The author's theatrical experience helps the example stories take on a life of their own.

CREATING STORIES FOR STORYTELLING
Marsh Cassady, PhD

Paper, 144 pages, 5½" x 8½", ISBN: 0-89390-205-5

This book picks up where the author's popular Storytelling Step-by-Step left off. Includes ideas for creating your own original stories, adapting stories to different audiences, plotting a story, creating tension, and writing dialogue that will keep your listeners on the edge of their chairs.

STORY AS A WAY TO GOD
A Guide for Storytellers

H. Maxwell Butcher

Paper, 153 pages, 5½" x 8½", ISBN: 0-89390-201-2

Why are stories so powerful? This book reveals the dynamics of good storytelling. Find out why every good story from "The Ugly American" to "West Side Story" says something about the divine. Learn how to find God's story everywhere, and how to tell it.

CRUSHED INTO GLORY
And Other Dramas for Preaching and Teaching

Joseph J. Juknialis and James Heimerl

Paper, 224 pages, 6" x 9", ISBN: 0-89390-340-X

Eighteen lectionary-based dramas that put the Word of God into a contemporary context. There are several dramas for each season and cycle of the church year. They are ready to help you tweak the imagination of people in your congregation. Use them as an occasional alternative to traditional preaching, in class, or with youth groups.

THREE-MINUTE DRAMAS FOR WORSHIP
Karen Patitucci

Paper, 261 pages, 5½" x 8½", ISBN: 0-89390-143-1

Here are 72 easy-to-memorize skits perfect for your church, classroom, or prayer group. The Bible-based dramas include theme and Scripture references that will help you decide which ones best fit your particular needs. Also includes tips on how to write and direct your own short dramas.

Order from your local bookseller, or contact:

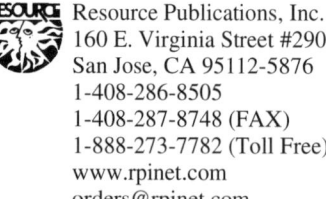

Resource Publications, Inc.
160 E. Virginia Street #290
San Jose, CA 95112-5876
1-408-286-8505
1-408-287-8748 (FAX)
1-888-273-7782 (Toll Free)
www.rpinet.com
orders@rpinet.com